They Made It!

How Chinese, French, German, Indian, Israeli and other foreign-born entrepreneurs contributed to high-tech innovation in Silicon Valley, the U.S. and Overseas

by Angelika Blendstrup, Ph.D.

HappyAbout.info

20660 Stevens Creek Blvd., Suite 210
Cupertino, CA 95014

First Printing: December 2007
Paperback ISBN: 1-60005-075-1
Place of Publication: Silicon Valley, California, U.S.
Paperback Library of Congress Number: 2007941246

eBook ISBN:1-60005-076-X

Trademarks

All terms mentioned in this book that are known to be trademarks or service marks have been appropriately capitalized. Happy About® cannot attest to the accuracy of this information. Use of a term in this book should not be regarded as affecting the validity of any trademark or service mark.

Warning and Disclaimer

Every effort has been made to make this book as complete and as accurate as possible, but no warranty of fitness is implied. The information provided is on an "as is" basis. The authors and the publisher shall have neither liability nor responsibility to any person or entity with respect to an loss or damages arising from the information contained in this book.

"Immigrants from Andy Grove to Vinod Koshla to Sergey Brin have made Silicon Valley the extraordinary success it is today. This book provides valuable lessons learned from the successful entrepreneurs that will prove inspiring to people from every country."

Steve Westly
Founder and CEO, The Westly Group,
Former California State Controller

"A fascinating book! Dr. Angelika Blendstrup has put together an accomplished and valuable composition on immigrants, their success and faith in progress. Her book portrays the American dream magnificently, or better said: the Silicon Valley dream."

Francois Dubrulle
Co-Founder and CEO, The Green Satellite

"Les experiences vecues ainsi decrites dans ce recueil d'interviews permettent de vraiment toucher du doigt le magique ecosystem de la Silicon Valley."

Bruno de Beauregard
Co-Founder and CEO, Netcipia

"If you are looking for the high road to success in business and in life...if you are fascinated by the Silicon Valley dream and the stories of people who have shaped it, you have found a unique guide with Angelika Blendstrup's new book."

"This book will help you stand on the shoulders of giants and remind you when you need it that anything is possible, that you can change the world and truly achieve your dreams."

Christian Forthomme
CEO, RealChange®, Aptos, California

"This is a wonderfully crafted book that illustrates the entrepreneurial spirit of America in general, and Silicon Valley in particular. Angelika's personal story, together with the inspirational tales of those interviewed, strikes a chord with all generations and communities collectively pursuing the American Dream."

Milan Mantri
Controller, Digital Chocolate
Cochair (Net-IP 2005)

"Many Europeans come to Silicon Valley drawn by the possibility of realizing their dreams and creating their own start-ups. The stories in this book by the international entrepreneurs of 'The Valley' are a valuable resource and will give these newly arrived business men and women insights they might not have received otherwise."

Caroline Raynaud
Managing Director, GABA
[German American Business Association]

"Reading this book, I really got the sense of what some of these successful folks went through. The greatest lesson is that most were able to rise to such great heights out of such ordinary beginnings. There wasn't any magic other than a desire to move forward toward a vision, and the willingness to work at it. This book will bring greatness to where you can see doing it and achieving it for yourself—i.e., changing the world is really not that unreachable after all—and that, IMHO, is the greatest take-away out of reading this book."

Scott SF Tse
Copresident of CSPA
www.cspa.com

Dedication

To my mother, who at 90 is still going strong. I thank her for her never-ending loving support and encouragement.

Acknowledgements

This book was a group effort. I could never have met all the entrepreneurs I interviewed, if it had not been for the help of my friends. Also, I was fortunate that many of the interviewees themselves referred me to their colleagues and friends, which led me to new and exciting people to talk to.

A very special, heart-felt thank you goes to my sister, Claudia [in real life, a lawyer] who transcribed all the interviews sitting at her computer for many months. I would not have gotten this far if she hadn't worked all these crazy hours.

My thanks in particular go to the Executive Assistants: Pam Shore (Google), Linda Norris (Allegis Capital), Carla Lindsay (Benhamou Global Ventures), Marilyn Ahern (Global Catalyst Partners), and Susan Schendel (The Honorable George Shultz), for the invaluable help they provided—and in such a very nice way.

My appreciation also goes to Sharon Turnoy, Senior Manager (Synopsys), Shanna Prevé, Executive Communications Advisor (Google), Korie Pelka, Senior Manager, Corporate Communications (EFI), and Katie Juran, Senior Manager, Corporate Public Relations (Adobe Systems).

Without the help of all these talented and dedicated professionals—who often went out of their way to help me—I would not have gotten back the interviews, nor the permission slips within the time frame I needed to.

Furthermore, *un grand merci* to Geraldine Reau, Susan Lucas-Conwell, Patti Wilson, Deborah Grove, Christina Yip Chung, Shirley Lin, Randy Hawks, Ian Griffin, Vladimir Jacimovic, Elisabetta Ghisini, Ale Gicqueau, Scott Tse, Walter Tijiboy, and Caroline Raynaud, who helped me either connect with someone else to continue the journey or stood by me with their enthusiasm and support.

Luckily I had met Mitchell Levy [my publisher, Happy About] a few years ago. He gave me the green light and assurance early on that he would publish this book.

Of course, my children hold an important, special place in this litany of thanks; my son Stephan and his new wife, Mira, for their enthusiasm in listening to me (smilingly) read aloud some of the chapters to get their feedback, and my daughter, Francisca, who sat with me, going through interview after interview—*just ten more minutes*—and pitched in with love, patience and expertise; she made my life and work so much easier.

A Message from Happy About®

Thank you for your purchase of this Happy About book. It is available online at http://happyabout.info/theymadeit.php or at other online and physical bookstores.

- Please contact us for quantity discounts at sales@happyabout.info
- If you want to be informed by e-mail of upcoming Happy About® books, please e-mail bookupdate@happyabout.info

Happy About is interested in you if you are an author who would like to submit a non-fiction book proposal or a corporation that would like to have a book written for you. Please contact us by e-mail editorial@happyabout.info or phone (1-408-257-3000).

Other Happy About books available include:

- I'm on LinkedIn--Now What???
  http://happyabout.info/linkedinhelp.php
- Happy About Online Networking
  http://happyabout.info/onlinenetworking.php
- Tales From the Networking Community
  http://happyabout.info/networking-community.php
- Awakening Social Responsibility
  http://happyabout.info/csr.php
- Scrappy Project Management
  http://happyabout.info/scrappyabout/project-management.php
- 42 Rules of Marketing
  http://happyabout.info/42rules/marketing.php
- Foolosophy
  http://happyabout.info/foolosophy.php
- The Home Run Hitter's Guide to Fundraising
  http://happyabout.info/homerun-fundraising.php
- Confessions of a Resilient Entrepreneur
  http://happyabout.info/confessions-entrepreneur.php
- Memoirs of the Money Lady
  http://happyabout.info/memoirs-money-lady.php
- 30-Day Bootcamp: Your Ultimate Life Makeover
  http://happyabout.info/30daybootcamp/life-makeover.php
- Rule #1: Stop Talking! A Guide to Listening
  http://happyabout.info/listenerspress/stoptalking.php
- Communicating the American Way
  http://happyabout.info/communicating-american-way.php

Contents

Silicon Valley: A Slice of Life

"The voyage of discovery is not in seeking new landscapes but in having new eyes."

Marcel Proust

Susan Lucas-Conwell, CEO, SDForum

It has been many years since the apricot trees disappeared from Palo Alto and the image of success became a garage in this idea economy. For those who think that silicon grows on the trees now... this is what it's really about [in 2007[1]]:

- Area: 1500 square miles (roughly San Jose to San Francisco)
- Population: 2.43 million
  - 38 percent foreign-born (of which 33 percent are Asian)
  - 50 percent speak a second+ language
  - 28 percent under 19 yrs old and 42 percent under 45 yrs old
  - 41 percent have college degrees

---

1. Statistics provided by the 2007 Index of Silicon Valley, Ref: www.jointventure.org

- 6600 tech companies employing 250k, market cap $450bn
- 284 tech workers per 1000 employees (vs. 51/1000 U.S. average)
- Highest level of R&D in the U.S.

And where's the money? Why do we care?

- **2005:** $8bn invested in 950 deals of which 1.6 percent in seed/start-ups ($132m in 47 deals)
- **2006:** $4.6b in 550 deals of which three percent in seed/start-ups ($130m in 40 deals)

This is all happening in an area with less than one percent of the U.S. population, an area that saw its first high-tech company in 1939 but was dominated by agriculture until 50 years ago.

What's the magic potion? The right ingredients and a chemical reaction...

The Circle of Innovation

- The entrepreneurial theater burgeoning with ideas and innovation.
- Mature firms = potential clients, partners, successful exits.
- Professional service providers and the support needed to grow these businesses. They are also invaluable partners and connectors in and of themselves.
- Institutions of higher learning are a source of knowledge, technology and research, employees, future entrepreneurs.
- Government plays a very different role here than in many countries. Cities can provide tax incentives, offices, incubators... All levels of government (city, state and federal) are potential customers of products and can be connectors at official levels among countries providing special incentives to different regions (e.g., NAFTA).

Contributions of SDForum

One of the crucial aspects of Silicon Valley is its networks; SDForum is one of the largest and oldest, representing a microcosm of the ecosystem for innovation. Created 23 years ago, SDForum is a non-profit dedicated to educating and creating relationships within the technology community, thus helping to transform innovation into scaleable businesses.

How does this network work? Here's an example:

- **Opelin**, an Indian Company (2003)
  - Developed in India
  - Opened office in Silicon Valley
  - Joined SDForum network to access investors, legal help, and industry thought leaders
  - Hired Silicon Valley-experienced CEO to help gain access to funding and customers
  - Raised $1M in Angel funding
  - Rolled out to 23 countries in 20 languages because of connections made
  - ...still going strong

As you read this fascinating collection of interviews, I hope this slice of life in Silicon Valley will come alive for you and make you realize what the reality of the Valley is: many, many new eyes bringing their vision and energy, their talents to create and innovate in a very special place. The people are what make the Valley tick, and they have come from everywhere in the world, all walks of life. This book mirrors what it's like for those looking inside.

Chapter 1

Introduction

First Impressions

Step out of the Arrivals Hall at San Francisco International Airport and you are faced with two choices. Head north to San Francisco, the Golden Gate Bridge, Fisherman's Wharf and other well-known tourist sites. Alternately, head south down the Peninsula toward Palo Alto, Mountain View, Cupertino and San Jose.

If you head south, you'll soon be in a typically American landscape of shopping centers, low-rise office buildings and shaded, suburban neighborhoods. But unlike similar neighborhoods on the outskirts of Dallas or Detroit, you are actually traveling through the global center of the high-technology industry—you are in Silicon Valley.

Extending south from the airport to San Jose and beyond, *The Valley* is home to companies such as Hewlett-Packard, Cisco, Sun Microsystems, eBay, Google, Yahoo! and thousands of others involved in creating the hardware and software of the digital age.

As much as the beauty of San Francisco is a magnet for tourists from around the world, the dynamism of Silicon Valley is a magnet for ambitious engineers, computer scientists, businesspeople and academics. The best and the brightest make their own way here, drawn to the unique opportunities found only in Silicon Valley.

The Interviewees

This book is a result of conversations I've had over the past 14 months with the leaders of Silicon Valley.

I didn't limit the interviews to the tried and true leaders of the Valley. I also talked to foreign leaders who touched Silicon Valley tangentially, but were just too interesting to leave out. They all do business in the U.S. and, as such, are relevant to the book.

Many of the people I spoke with chose to leave their homes, fly to the U.S. (often for their college education) and, in due time, land at SFO and drive south. The foreign-born interviewees (some permanent immigrants; others not) are from around the world: China, France, Germany, India, Israel and elsewhere.

To get an American perspective on the impact of foreign input in the high-tech sector, I talked to some key American members of the Silicon Valley community.

The majority of people in this book, whether foreign- or U.S.-born, made a conscious decision—earlier or later in life—to engage with Silicon Valley.

My Story

I am one of these people. I am an immigrant myself. Even if my life does not compare to the lives of the executives I interviewed, I come from the same perspective. I came to the U.S. as an adult for my higher education, and I have found fulfillment in my life and work here in Silicon Valley.

After undergraduate studies at the University of Tuebingen, Germany, I came to UC Berkeley and received my Master's Degree in Comparative Literature. I studied for my Ph.D. in Education at Stanford University.

I now live in Palo Alto, in the heart of Silicon Valley. And, in my own way, I make a small impact on the lives around me. I have my own company, Blendstrup & Associates, teaching accent reduction, presentation and cross-cultural skills to leading foreign-born engineers, executives and entrepreneurs from around the world. Not only do I work with the smartest, most motivated people, but I can also directly see how they gain more confidence and progress in their communication skills, making their lives in the U.S. happier and richer.

In addition, I teach classes at Stanford University on cross-cultural skills, management of virtual teams, and the elements of successful interviews. For those readers who are interested in doing business here in the U.S., and feel they need more insight into U.S. business practices, please consult the book I co-authored with my colleague Elisabetta Ghisini, *Communicating the American Way.*

Why this Book

Hearing the stories of the executives I met at Silicon Valley networking events inspired me to write this book. I started by interviewing French executives I met through the InterFrench business association. I then found other fascinating foreign-born entrepreneurs—at the peak of their success or striving toward it—who shared their stories with me. And so I began the serendipitous journey of being handed off from one person to the next within the international community of The Valley.

The first decade of the 21st Century is an appropriate time to review the contributions of immigrants and other foreign-born professionals to Silicon Valley. As the 2007 Silicon Valley Index reports:

Over half of the region's science and engineering (S&E) talent was born abroad...Foreign-born talent in Silicon Valley represents roughly three times the national shares in S&E and in all occupations...A critical component to assessing a region's talent base in today's economy is in its ability to attract talent from other countries. Despite the economic downturn after 2000, Silicon Valley has continued to draw talent from abroad.[2]

Since I was around so many unique, varied intellects, I wanted to understand what it is that draws this special kind of talent from around the world to this small corner of America at the southern end of the San Francisco Bay. What are the unique challenges and opportunities which attract people to this habitat for innovation and entrepreneurship? [3] What motivated many of the entrepreneurs to move to a foreign country—a country they knew only from stories or from television—often without funds or jobs waiting for them? What passions drove them to do another start-up, or to take a position at a new company? How do they handle wealth? What mark do they want to leave on society?

I wanted to hear people's stories first-hand. I wanted to hear from the people who made it here. I wish I could have reprinted all the interviews in full. But in the interest of space, a content editor had to do a full edit of the printed version. You can read extra material and stories from the interviews (and five additional, full interviews) on my website: http://www.professional-business-communications.com.

If you are interested in the big picture, the economy, the companies, then you can, of course, use one of Silicon Valley's well-known inventions and Google for the data.

But I would like to invite you to listen to the experiences of some of the foreign-born entrepreneurs who helped make Silicon Valley, in their own words. I invite you to join with me and listen to fascinating conversations with Silicon Valley greats as they discuss what makes one successful and what ingredients are necessary to be a good leader. One interviewee, Raj Singh, defined success as *being like an anti-oxidant* (read Raj's interview in The Start-Up Wizards).

This is not a book with a lot of editorial interpretation. The words of the interviewees speak for themselves.

---

2. Joint Venture, 2007 Index of Silicon Valley, San Jose, 11.

3. Lee, C.M. et al, The Silicon Valley Edge: a Habitat for Innovation and Entrepreneurship, Stanford University Press, 2000.

Role Models

The majority of people profiled in this book are foreign-born professionals who have made significant contributions in their fields. These are people at the top of their game.

Of course Silicon Valley is not only full of incredible foreigners who have left their imprint. Many Americans came here too, and together with their foreign counterparts, built companies.

The reason I included American entrepreneurs, dignitaries and academics in the book is because I wanted to see how much they were conscious of the role foreign contributions had made to their own success and to the development of the Valley and the U.S. in general.

I hope that the personal and professional advancements of the foreign entrepreneurs will inspire you, just as they acknowledge their debt to mentors and role models. Most agree they could not have made it to where they are now anywhere else and are grateful for the chances the Valley, and this country, have given them.

There's a lot to be learned from the people I talked to. You might learn the importance of approaching bright colleagues around you and starting your own company. You might learn how to parlay your foreign background to your advantage by teaming up with others from your country and culture. You might even learn from the interviewees' mistakes. Not all these leaders coasted along the path to their highest peaks. They—as we all do—had their highs and lows. Many successful people in Silicon Valley embrace the lessons of failure (and often feel you haven't really earned your stars if you haven't had at least one failure). You, in turn, might be able to save yourself from a couple of failures by heeding the lessons in these stories.

Networking

I selected people to interview in typical Silicon Valley fashion.

One of the distinctive features of Silicon Valley is how approachable people are: "relationships and even gossip (are) a crucial aspect of... business." [4]

I had networked for many years, going to international business events weekly (starting in 1997 with the Silicon Valley Internet Center where 130 people met weekly to talk about IT and their own start-ups).

Over the years, I made many international contacts; they in turn often became friends. I started my interviews with the French executives I already knew; they quickly made themselves available to me and gave me referrals to their contacts. Then I turned to Chinese, Israeli and Indian leaders who not only let me interview them, but sent emails to their friends encouraging them to talk to me as well. A few of the interviews, of necessity, were conducted by telephone. Most were face-to-face meetings, and most importantly, they let me ask them probing questions and I kept to our allotted time!

It took various amounts of time to secure an interview. Some were conducted within a week of my initial request. Others took months to arrange. These are very busy people and I was conscious of the need to respect their time. In fact, when I was talking to the Chairman and CEO of Synopsys, Aart de Geus, I literally jumped up at the end of our (30-minute) time and dashed out of his office so he could take an incoming important phone call (luckily we did get to the last question).

I interviewed people in coffee shops; their offices; in their board rooms.

All of the interviewees took the time to go through their transcripts, some making major changes, others only doing some fact correcting, but each of them gave me back the corrected version with their permission to publish.

I was amazed that these stellar people would give me their time (this is the scarcest commodity in Silicon Valley) and whenever I left, I marveled at the interviewees—and I hoped some of their wisdom and creativity would rub off on me.

Once I sat down with the person, the interviews lasted anywhere from 30 minutes to two hours; most were 45 minutes long. This is reflected in the different lengths of many chapters. Even though I had a pre-de-

---

4. Saxenian, AL., Regional Advantage: Culture and Cooperation in Silicon Valley and Route 128, Harvard University Press, 1994, 33.

fined set of questions (see Appendix A), I did not try to control each conversation, letting it go wherever it wanted to.

Some are detailed biographies of a person; others brief portraits of a moment in time. I hope that they will entertain and inform you. If you are intrigued by the people you hear and would like to meet types like them personally, simply come to Silicon Valley and attend business networking meetings. You might meet them at the next Interfrench/SiliconFrench, TIE, HYSTA, HISPANIC-NET, SIPA, CSPA, SDForum, NetIP or GABA events.

Silicon Valley Today

Just as there are no *typical* interviews, there are no *typical* Silicon Valley companies. It is pointless to make generalizations that apply across the board. This is an area defined by diversity: in technology (from nanotechnology to search engines; from contract manufacturing to genetic engineering); in business models (from Fortune 50 companies to the proverbial start-up in a garage); in people (from the All-American man or woman to people from a wide range of ethnic backgrounds). Some data points:

- The City of Fremont reports over 100 different languages are spoken by students at home.[5]
- Immigrant-founded venture-backed public companies employ an estimated 220,000 people in the United States.[6]
- Foreign households moving to Silicon Valley rose by 15 percent in 2004-2005.[7]

---

5. City of Fremont, 2006 Visitors Guide, 10.

6. Anderson, S. and M. Platzer, *American Made: The Impact of Immigrant Entrepreneurs and Professionals on U.S. Competitiveness*, National Venture Capital Association (NVCA), 2006, 7.

7. Joint Venture, 2007 Index of Silicon Valley, San Jose, 2007, 6.

The Foreign-Born Entrepreneurs

All people who decide to move to the U.S. have made a huge transition in their lives. The uncertainty and lack of predictability involved in emigration or resettling overseas to work or study means that there's a self-selecting process at work. Many people who are willing to leave their homes and move abroad are, by definition, more tolerant of risk and more adventurous than their fellow countrymen.

It also means that immigrants/foreign-born professionals are often different from the native-born Americans they live among. They differ in accent and attitude, culture and commitment. Distinct differences come across time and again in my interviews.

Each reader will react to the interviews in different ways. Some of you might not agree with the *strange* attitudes toward work, family and leisure (e.g., the 24/7 work culture). Others might see parts of themselves in these profiles. If you live outside of the U.S.—perhaps planning how to make your own way to Silicon Valley—you will have a different reaction to the stories from people who live here already. You might see a role model. You might see a way to realize your own dreams. *Chacun à son goût.*

The people I interviewed came to the U.S. under different circumstances. Each person responded to different factors in his/her unique biography, education and geography. Yet what strikes me after recording and editing these interviews are the common threads that run through the stories.

These are motivated, ambitious, driven people. They are not afraid of hard work. They see opportunity where others see difficulty. But in spite of impossible hours, they still see the importance of family and make a point of including their spouses and children.

Each person I talked to is unique; therefore I could not see the sense in grouping him or her by country or nationality. I thought I could best present their stories by grouping them into different categories.

The Interviews—Major Categories

The participants in the book are typically hard to place; many of the VCs were CEOs or start-up specialists and are now at another place in their lives. For example, John Hennessy, the President of Stanford University, could be placed under start-up wizard, engineer, academic entrepreneur or CEO. After much debate, I decided to go with the executives' current roles in life and create categories to suit them.

In the Appendices, besides the list of questions asked, there is a list of universities the interviewees attended.

Creating this book has given me a unique perspective on Silicon Valley. Each person's story is a different view into the relationship among technological innovation, entrepreneurship, risk-taking, plain hard work, and how these have played a role in forming their lives. Feel free to read just those stories that interest you. If you read one chapter or the whole book, I hope that you'll begin to understand the different ways success can be achieved in Silicon Valley. And then begin to write your own chapter.

Chapter 2

The VCs

Venture capitalists not only provide financing for start-up companies, they also broker influential social networks and play the role of corporate advisors, recruiters and management consultants. They truly are the coaches of Silicon Valley. They often succeed as much because of their informal networks of advisors whom they can bring to the party as by their knowledge of technology.

Foreign-born VCs have a unique perspective. Often having made their initial fortune by entrepreneurship, they are attuned to the potential of fellow immigrant professionals as well as knowing the land of high tech and the U.S. business culture. Their understanding of the nuances of different cultures together with their practical business knowledge makes for a formidable combination. These people tell the stories of the Venture Capitalists:

- Eric Benhamou, Chairman and CEO, Benhamou Global Ventures
- Jean-Louis Gassée, General Partner, Allegis Capital

- Henry Wong, Founder and Managing Director, Diamond Venture Technology
- Eric Buatois, Managing Partner, Sofinnova

Eric Benhamou, Chairman and CEO, Benhamou Global Ventures

Eric Benhamou
Founder and CEO, Benhamou Global Ventures
Country of Origin: France
Group: The VCs

> *"I used to say that you have to sell your vision one pixel at a time."*

Eric Benhamou is part of a network of individuals who are accomplished high-tech professionals and are at the point in their career where they want to give something back to society. To get some balance in his busy life, he runs marathons.

New Directions

Q: *What you are currently doing?*

A: For the past three years, I have moved into a different phase of my professional career. I no longer run companies, private or public. I basically help others build successful companies, technology companies. My approach is not to make passive investments, but to make active investments.

That's one of the things I do. I call it BGV, Benhamou Global Ventures. Another thing I do is, I teach.

Teaching at INSEAD

Q: *Where?*

A: At INSEAD, in France. It is a very global business school and has a different mindset than for example, Stanford, where I went. I find it attractive, because the students tend to be mature, motivated and more diversified. In my first course, I had 50 students representing 13 different countries. The average age was almost 30. It was very enjoyable, because I could tell the people were really there for a purpose. They wanted to get the most out of it. There was more diversity of perspectives presented in a case discussion than I ever experienced at Stanford.

Israel Venture Network

The third part is, I do a lot more work in non-profit activities. A few years ago I started a venture philanthropy network called IVN, which stands for "The Israel Venture Network" and this is basically a network of individuals who are accomplished professionals, mostly from the high tech field, and are at the point in their career where they want to give something back to society. It's not just money, it's mostly in fact an approach to problem solving. They have a way of dispassionately understanding problems, analyzing root causes, making rational decisions based on data, measuring the progress, creating feedback loops, creating dashboard and measurement systems, setting clear goals and measuring progress against those goals.

Those are things that you take for granted when you build a business, which are remarkably absent from non-profit programs or government programs.

Childhood Influences

Q: *How did your childhood experiences or your family influence you to where you are today?*

A: I was born in a small village on the border between Algeria and Morocco, in 1955. This was at a time when there were independence wars brewing through the region and we had to leave the country in 1960 along with about 500,000 other people.

I think this helped me with learning to uproot myself and leave everything behind and restart with nothing; it demystifies the experience, in other words. For many people, the prospect of doing this is devastating, but if you do this early in your life and realize, okay, this is just part of my life, you survive, you move on, you build a new environment and build new friends.

I had a good family environment, but the sort of things that you now see on TV—you see schools and hospitals being blown up—was basically the environment I grew up in. My school was bombed, my house was bombed. I remember going back from school to my apartment. I had to avoid some blocks where there had been terrorist attacks.

I can really identify with the world we live in today. But the plus side of living through this when you are a 3...4...5 year old kid, it gets you prepared for many of the challenges of the rest of your life.

Then moving from Paris to Silicon Valley was really very straightforward. I was not traumatized by this change, it was a wonderful experience.

Q: *Wait, wait, in between, you jumped. So you went from Algeria to Morocco to Paris.*

A: Actually to Grenoble. I went to high school there. Then I went to Paris. I grew up as a teenager in France. My native culture is a combination of French and North African culture.

Q: *Were your parents well educated?*

A: They were both professors, so when they moved from Algeria to France, I've always been close to a school environment. All of this helped me. This experience of moving and leaving everything behind is great. It prepares you to be an entrepreneur, because an entrepreneur has to be able to leave everything behind and start from scratch and climb a new hill that has never been climbed before. In that sense, it is very exhilarating. If you can look at the positive challenge aspect of it, you not only survive, you thrive.

Motivation to Leave France

Q: *What was the motivation for you to leave France for the United States?*

A: There were a couple of things which turned me off in my experiences in France. One was an attitude of extreme conservatism and the discouragement of entrepreneurs. I was much more entrepreneurially oriented than the ambient culture.

I didn't feel comfortable there; there was also anti-Semitism. I didn't feel comfortable as a young Jewish teenager and so I came to this country to have a new experience. It was so totally positive that I knew within a few weeks of being here, I was going to spend a lot of time here.

Stanford Graduate Studies

Q: *Where did you come to first?*

A: I went to Stanford as a graduate student in the School of Engineering.

I had a good skill set in putting problems into equations and abstracting things. This is a very transportable skill. You can apply this to many different fields. It turns out when I was here, the world was discovering microprocessors and network communications. Stanford is very close to Xerox PARC and there were a lot of discoveries made there. These migrated through the Stanford research community very quickly, in fact, it was the same community—just a few miles apart—and I was exposed to it very early and it had an influence on my career.

When I first came to this country, I thought I was going to study biomedical engineering. After a few months here, I became much more taken by the emerging field of microcomputers, the emergence of network communications.

Q: *That was very early and you were really ahead of the curve.*

Early Days of the Internet

A: Yes, it was early. They did not call that the Internet, but can you imagine in 1975 having an email address with an @ sign and being able to speak to people at SRI?

Q: *Yes, but only because I heard Vinton Cerf speak at CSPA and he is giving me an interview too. Those must have been incredible times.*

A: Vint Cerf was there, of course. This was the first era of the Internet before it was called by this name.

Q: *Was there an aura of excitement about it, did you realize the big thing it was going to be, or was it just interesting?*

A: I don't think any of us realized how big a thing it was going to be in the end. But we all knew that we were onto the beginning of something totally new and unexplored, and we knew that an industry was going to be built on this. That is what inspired me in my first jobs and the first companies that I started. It had a profound influence on what I ended up doing throughout my career.

Obstacles

Q: *What were the biggest obstacles in your past that you had to overcome?*

A: Well, what I found difficult to overcome I wouldn't call it difficulties, but it took me a few years to master this. If you want to be successful in business you have to be passionate and dispassionate at the same time. You have to be very passionate about your goals and your ambitions and your vision but at the same time you have to be totally dispassionate in how you analyze problems. You have to be totally objective.

As we say in Silicon Valley, "You have to learn not to drink your own Kool Aid." If you drink your own Kool Aid, you lose your sense of objectivity. You have to be able to turn this on at the right moment.

Success

Q: *What does it mean to you to be successful?*

A: I feel successful when I am accomplishing things that I once thought impossible, which I had set as a lofty distant objective. So if you are able to accomplish and go beyond that, you are feeling your success. Today I am experiencing this vicariously because I am trying to inspire other people to reach beyond their own limits.

I have experienced this in companies I have built. My longest tenure as a CEO was in 3Com where I was until Dec. 2000. This was a fun ride.

Of course it was stressful along the way. We had the feeling that it was our generation. It was our generation at the prime of our careers when the Internet was being built. It's a unique challenge. It was the challenge of our generation, and we were going to give the Internet to the world and we were building the components for it. I learned the protocols from Vint Cerf at Stanford and he was later building this in commercial products and for large corporations all over the world. In the '80s, our goal was to connect one million people to the networks during the decade.

The '80s rolled by and we had connected 10 million people. In the '90s we were going to be even more ambitious. We were going to try to connect 100 million people. The '90s rolled by and when I stepped down as CEO, we had connected 400 million people to networks.

It was an incredible ride being able to exceed our most ambitious objectives.

Uniqueness of Silicon Valley

Q: *Could you have been successful outside of Silicon Valley?*

A: No, I don't even hesitate a second on this. This was a unique environment. This is a land of entrepreneurship by definition. I was trusted by investors in a way that I would not have been trusted anywhere else. I was trusted to lead a large company before I had even proven myself as a CEO. I was trusted to turn around a business even though there were a lot of people who, on paper, were better qualified.

Q: *What do you attribute that to?*

A: I think I was fortunate to deal with colleagues and investors who could sense my entrepreneurial commitment, my total commitment to the vision of the company. And they felt I was a good fit. Sometimes fire overcomes experience.

Challenges for Multicultural Leadership

Q: *What are the greatest challenges you see in a multicultural leadership role?*

A: Well, actually I experienced that much earlier than now. In the early '90s, my company was totally global. We started to make acquisitions all over the globe. We didn't care about the nationalities, religions or skin colors of the employees. We cared about their competence. So to me, it has always been obvious that the companies we are building are meritocracies. There is a common culture in this industry that is far stronger than the differences that exist at birth or by education. I never found this to be a problem.

Leadership Skills

Q: *What are the three most important things to be a good leader?*

A: The first thing without which you can't speak about leadership is you have to have a vision about an inspiring future whether it is in a business environment or whatever your field happens to be. You have to have a vision which is substantially more inspiring and enabling than the reality of today. You have to have that. You have to visualize it clearly in your mind and you have to have a commitment to it. Without that you can't lead people.

I think the second thing that is absolutely essential is that you have to have total integrity; if you make compromises with this vision, or if you are not totally committed to your relationships, to high integrity relationships, there will be flaws in your relationships. And, you won't be effective as a leader if you are not honest with yourself and with the people you work with every day.

The third thing is: If you want to inspire others, you have to be an effective communicator. That doesn't mean that you have to be a super charismatic speaker, but people have to believe you and they have to understand the depth of your commitment.

Q: *What about communication skills?*

A: I used to say that you have to sell your vision one pixel at a time. It requires perseverance, persistence and, at every encounter, you must convince people on a one-on-one basis.

You meet people in small groups and large groups. With every encounter you make progress, more of the vision gets communicated, and more people rally to your cause. So it requires endurance. You have to show patience and understand that there will be setbacks on the way, but the more you invest in this communication, the more will rally around your cause. It is particularly important when you turn around a company.

Advice for Foreign-Born Entrepreneurs

Q: *What advice would you give, not necessarily only to the French, but to young foreign-born entrepreneurs who live here or who come here to make it?*

A: I think it would dovetail with the three things that we just talked about. They have to believe in themselves, because without that belief you can't build anything that matters. You remember the *Indiana Jones* movie where you have to cross the precipice; you have to put your foot onto the ledge.

Q: *The swinging bridge?*

A: No, not the swinging bridge, the bridge was invisible. He closes his eyes; you have to believe. You put your foot in the void only to find a ledge to support you. So there are going to be a lot of these moments in your leadership journey where you have to be inspired to take a risk, not knowing if there is a net to catch you. If you are unable to do that, if you need to have many nets visible to you, you don't have the risk-taking ability to accomplish great things.

To me, that's a core ingredient. If you don't have it, then maybe you're not destined to be an entrepreneur, you're not destined to be a leader. That's okay, not everyone needs to do that. You can have completely full lives without doing this.

Jean-Louis Gassée, General Partner, Allegis Capital

Jean-Louis Gassée
General Partner, Allegis Capital
Country of Origin: France
Group: The VCs

> *"I love what I do, I do what I love,* ***and*** *I get paid for it."*

Jean-Louis Gassée is one of the most interesting, truly unique men I have met. He is familiar with any business topic and his knowledge of the world in general is quite incredible.

Q: *How would you describe what you do professionally today?*

A: Well, there are two ways. One is a more traditional way. I support the ambitions of entrepreneurs—mostly it takes the form of money but also advice or putting together a strategy to build a team. We help build high-tech companies. And in doing so, we make money for two constituencies: one is the entrepreneur whom we serve, and the other our limited partners, the investors. That's what we do and it's heaven. The other part of my description would be that all of my past mistakes are assets to the firm.

Q: *How did your childhood experiences or your family influence you in your life or choice of career?*

A: My family, like many families, was not the easiest one. I had to drop out of school because of family troubles. I also had all sorts of jobs, from being a bartender in a very nice, very chic bar in Deauville to being a *maitre d'* in a street joint in Montparnasse. I also sold pharmaceuticals, office equipment and insurance. I worked at the railway company, and finally that ended when I joined Hewlett-Packard and came back into civilization.

Q: *Had you gone to a Grande École?* [Elite French university focused on engineering, business or humanities]

A: No. I was on my way there when trouble struck. To be fair, that was probably a good thing. I'm not the Grande École type. I'm too independent and rebellious. Those four years where I worked at odd jobs were immensely helpful because when I came to HP, I knew I had arrived. I remember June 24, 1968, when I joined HP and I said, "That's it, I have arrived—in a very real sense." I joined that company and it was such a wonderful company. They were very tolerant of the angry young man. It was great because all I had to do was continue. I had found the high-tech world, I loved it, and that was it.

Q: *What were some of the challenges you had to overcome in the high-tech world?*

A: If I were arrogant, I would say I just had to row the boat. The greatest challenge I had to overcome was to calm down. I remember the way I treated people at HP when I joined. It's amazing that they put up with me. Of course, you have to be realistic and produce some results. People still have good memories of me because I was a little out of the ordinary and I got things done.

Q: *Which leads me of course to Apple. Steve Jobs can be annoying it is said, but he, of course, produces. Did you enjoy Apple? Was it a challenge?*

A: Well yes, it was the best and the worst of times. Building everything up "was a ball." When I signed my employment agreement with Apple, December 12,1980, in Geneva, at a restaurant called Le Duc—an outpost of a very famous fish restaurant in Paris in Montparnasse—I said, "If I can hire two other people, I'm done."

And actually, I hired three people, the two I had in mind from HP and a third I had found at IBM—Jean Calmon (you've met him) who is a marvelous sales executive. They knew what to do, they were very good. And then, in turn, because they were very good, they hired good people. For some reason we found a way to merge the Californian culture of Apple with the French view of the world. That was wonderful. That got me recruited to Cupertino, to a lot of project development, R&D and then to be the President of the Project Division and then to being fired. They were difficult times. I hated the corporate politics. I hated them and I wasn't pleasant.

Q: *What does it mean to you to be successful, and what factors contributed to your success?*

A: Success to me means doing something that, figuratively speaking, when you knock it, it gives off a good sound. What the French call a *son plein*, a nicer sound. No *zings*, you know, a nice sound. It could be a nice product, it could be building a nice company, and it could be having a successful family.

Q: *Or a combination of all those?*

A: To me, it's a combination of all those. Being successful is not a state. We know the epistemological difficulties of the present. What is the present? But without digging into that I say, to me, it's moving in life with a feeling of glowing. There's the family side, the financial side, the spiritual side, seeing some milestones either behind or in front of you. To me, it's doing a good job as a human being. If you want to summarize, it's doing a good job as a human being. That can be big, that can be small.

Q: *Could you have been as successful outside Silicon Valley?*

A: No. No, Silicon Valley is heaven. It is! It is what I call the united nations, small 'u', small 'n' of Silicon Valley. The color of your skin, the turban you wear or not, the veil you wear, the keypad, your accent, the color of your passport, the way you lead your private life, your lifestyle which is in plain English, they way you make love, with whom you make love. It doesn't matter what you do, it's what you *can* do!

Q: *Right, how creative are you?*

A: Interestingly, I've had this discussion with many French self-appointed judges of the United States, and I mentioned to them that there is a spiritual side to the Silicon Valley. It's what you talked about as American materialism. I think the best column I ever wrote for *Liberation* was one called *Ah, le bon vieux materialism!* Ah, the good old materialism! It is where I stated what I fear in the U.S. is not materialism, it's religion, as opposed to spirituality. This is a very spiritual place. How many Zen Monasteries do you have from Marin County to Esalen? How many Baha'i temples? So, it's a spiritual side to Silicon Valley that I also enjoy.

Q: *Did your French background give you any advantages or disadvantages?*

A: Both. The French are characterized/stereotyped as being abrasive and arrogant. And that is true.

Q: *But not the ones living here, right?*

A: After a while, no, because otherwise they would get expelled. People tell me, "Look, look, the French people flourish in Silicon Valley." You know, you have a selection; the ones who don't flourish, you don't see because they go back and you don't see them anymore.

Q: *What are the greatest challenges for multicultural leadership today?*

A: None, none, there is no great challenge. I mean seriously, it is easy here. One of the best things that humans do is to guess the rule. That is how we learn speech, we guess. Okay, so you come here and if you are destined to survive, you guess what the rule is. And once you guess what the rule is, there is no challenge from the multicultural leadership.

Q: *What is the most important thing you need as a leader, and what are the negative things—all in one?*

A: Well, the negative thing is easy.

Q: *Arrogance?*

A: Well, no. Steve Jobs is arrogant. Larry Ellison is arrogant. So, arrogance is way undervalued. Arrogance is unpleasant, but that is not an issue to be a leader. You know people follow Steve Jobs because he is arrogant, because he gives the speech that moves people to action. All right, of course, arrogance is unpleasant. Let's not confuse things. Being a leader is not the same thing as being pleasant. It is not a necessary condition to being a leader. Look at all the great leaders: De Gaulle, Churchill. The great obstacles to leadership are too much insecurity, too much selfishness, confusion, the obvious things. Now, there are two kinds of leaders.

A: Picture this in physics: You put iron filings on a piece of paper and the magnet under it. You see the iron filings organize themselves along the lines of the magnetic field. That's one kind of leader, the magnet. Then, in another experiment, you create a uniform magnetic field, you shake the filings and they organize themselves in nice parallel lines. Take a piece of non-magnetic iron, you put it under the piece of paper and what happens? You see the lines of filings organize themselves as if the non-magnetic piece of iron were magnetic. This is because the non-magnetic piece of iron is diamagnetic; it facilitates the flow of the magnetic field, and this is another kind of leader.

Q: *How do you translate that into human qualities?*

A: It is a leader who just facilitates, channels, organizes and helps the energy of others. Leadership can oscillate between the two. Sometimes being the magnet, sometimes being the facilitator, and that's the ideal.

Q: *If you weren't doing what you are doing right now, what else would you have liked to do?*

A: I don't know. Well, I'd be an entrepreneur, I'd be in the high-tech business because that's what I like. To this day, after more than 30 years in the high-tech world, I still chuckle: *I love what I do, I do what I love and I get paid for it.*

I'd be an entrepreneur, not a *corpocrat*. I like what I do, this is heaven because I have the spiritual and the material rewards rolled into the same joint.

Q: *What advice would you give to the French, who are either living or coming here?*

A: It's not for everyone. Love it and, if you can't love it, leave it. Understand the system, don't be judgmental; it's okay to be judgmental, but for only two and a half minutes. Don't be judgmental.

Q: *So how do you get ahead, what's the secret sauce?*

A: Don't try. Just don't think of getting ahead, think of having fun. Or let me put it another way; when I was 25 years old I had a small epiphany: you don't make enough. I look at the person in front of me, she doesn't make enough. What can I do? And if you really behave like this enough of the time, you'll do fine. Because if you're really thinking enough of how you can help your boss make more money, trust me, you'll do just fine. Try to help other people get ahead!

Q: *What about entrepreneurs if they want to make it?*

A: Well, they have customers, they have employees, and they have investors, basically. They don't make enough, your employees don't make enough, and your investors don't make enough and your customers don't make enough, what can you do?

Q: *Do you focus more on the product or the customers' side, i.e., where is your energy?*

A: As an old shrink used to say: "I know you can do excellent things for the wrong reasons." The best part of us sometimes is in the dark side because it provides the drive, the creativity. What's the difference between anger and creativity? Well, use your dark side and channel it to creativity.

Q: *Fabulous! Anything else I should ask you? I love your stories Jean-Louis. [laughter]*

A: Thank you, flattery always works on me, keep going...

Q: *You know you are very respected in Silicon Valley, Jean-Louis.*

A: You know, I'm a recovering assoholic!

Q: *With that answer, the question was worth it!*

A: I love what I do, what can I say. People ask me—you know I'm 62— "When are you going to retire?" I say "What for?" So, I have fun. Behind the whole idea of retirement is that people were miserable—les damnés de la terre—as the old Internationale hymn says, so to speak; we are past—most of us here—where work is damnation.

Q: *I think that's what makes Silicon Valley so special. You meet everyone around you, nobody complains; it's fun, everyone listens to you, challenges your creativity, gives you more ideas; for me, that's what's amazing here.*

A: So, if you dreaded work and then stopped working, you could have fun. But if you have fun at work, work is life. And we have ample free time—no, it's great.

Henry Wong, Founder and Managing Director, Diamond Venture Technology

Henry H. Wong
Founder and Managing Director of Diamond Tech Ventures
Country of Origin: Hong Kong, China
Group: The VCs

> *"If you can present an idea, a concept, a technical piece that excels—you win. I don't care who you are, you're Martian, I don't care. Bring me the end result; bring me something we can all use."*

Henry is one of those serial entrepreneurs who live up to high-tech myths; he really designed a start-up on a napkin (but not in a garage). What is fun for him is being the (unofficial) Iron Chef not only of Beijing, but also of Silicon Valley.

Q: *What you are doing professionally today?*

A: I'm a venture capitalist by trade right now. As a VC, you have to make sure that the entrepreneurs are executing on a weekly and monthly basis and don't slip a month without telling you.

Early History

Q: *How did your childhood and your family contribute to your path in life to move you to where you are today?*

A: I was born and raised in Hong Kong. I was adventurous when I was a kid. In fact, after I came to America to study, I wanted to do my MBA in Telecom Management from Golden Gate University. They have a School of the Future program. I was really into the futuristic kind of things.

In 1979, when I graduated with my Bachelor's Degree from the University of Utah in Salt Lake City, I applied for graduate school and at the same time, I applied for jobs. I had many offers but I went to Burroughs in San Jose. The branch manager made me an offer, and I took it. I thought that computers were the future, and here I am in Silicon Valley.

Job Moves

Q: *And what happened then after you were at Burroughs?*

A: Burroughs at that time was selling a grand concept named BNA, Burroughs Network Architecture, similar to the IBM SNA. Very exciting, networking stuff. They had a mainframe in the middle of several super media minicomputers around the world and they were communicating with the mainframe. This is purely for Fortune 500 companies and Burroughs did a very good job in that.

Q: *Does it still exist?*

A: Burroughs still exists, it's now Unisys, they merged. After that I went to Rolm. It's a computerized PBX company founded by Ken Oshman. I learned a lot from him. I was totally energized. I must credit some of my energy as being inherited from Rolm: the positive mental thinking, the motivation, the go-getter type, that's from them.

Q: *Are these American qualities, or Silicon Valley / American qualities?*

A: It's what you call the Silicon Valley process. Some of the management came from the original Xerox professional selling class, so they certainly learned a lot from there and continued to refine it the California way. It's the U.S., but California is not really a good representation of the U.S., I'm sorry, but you can't find this attitude and work ethics back East or in the Midwest. There, if you work 18 hour days, they would say "Oh, you're so weird." In Silicon Valley, here, it's different, it's the difference between winning and losing. As an engineer, you are welcome to sleep under your desk and not go home for the night, but just wait for your recompile.

Being number one or number two is being very, very aggressive here. It is very competitive. Here they walk faster, talk faster, they demand that the computer respond right now. I wish I had two computers on my desk. My brother has three. I could be doing one thing on one computer, another thing on another.

At night time you may be doing something programming-wise, you may be doing something on your desk and then you send over a program to India, or to China to the software department and they will compile it and clean it up for you; you are parallel processing, using one brilliant brain for two tasks you can easily handle. That saves you time. While in some other country they only work 20 days a month.

Q: *So after you went to Rolm, what then?*

A: After Rolm, I went to Digital Equipment Corp. I was totally technically trained in the CAD-CAM industry. The only good thing about them is that for every four weeks that you work, one week out of that time will be training.

Q: *How long did you work there?*

A: I was at DEC a couple of years, and it was very, very good training.

Then one of the original founders of the Ethernet jumped ship and formed his own company, Telenova. They were located in Los Gatos. They addressed the fifth-generation PBX space and that was one step beyond Rolm. I was very excited. Also, they have a pre-ISDN backplane 2B+D.

Q: *What did you do there?*

A: I was in charge of the Western region. Wang Laboratories liked it so much that Dr. Wang came in and bought the company. I was transferred to the Wang regional office, running the Western region.

First Venture

Some people at AMD and National Semiconductor taped out a chip set, and finally I decided to start my own company called ISDN Systems.

Q: *When was that?*

A: That was 1988. And then in 1989, I invited a friend of a friend in to become the CEO in the company so he could run the company for me. In 1988, I was only a kid, I really wasn't eligible to be CEO.

In fact I walked up and down Sand Hill Road and a VC told me, one very nice guy, "You know Henry, you are a bright guy, but no one will invest money with you unless you have a real CEO. You are a first time CEO and VCs don't pay for training. In fact, they don't pay for a CEO in training."

And that's true, why should you bet your money on a horse that is not proven? You should bet on a horse that has won a couple of battles before. There is good reasoning behind it. Now I am on the "dark side," the other side, whatever they say [general laughter].

You have to bet on an entrepreneur who has the enthusiasm and the guts and the get-go who wants to do it. You may replace him or make sure that he understands that when the company gets more mature you will get someone to formulate and execute procedures and skill sets that will help you. These kinds of people are very useful and we should never diminish their fever or the quest for success. That was me in 1988, but that's okay. I learned a lot from that CEO and that company turned out to be Combinet.

Combinet was sold to Cisco in a stock swap worth $165 million. But the success story doesn't end there yet. Cisco split five times.

Q: *Did you get any money out of that?*

A: Lots of money, but it was anti-climatic. When I got the stock certificate it didn't mean much. It was just a piece of paper. I just said, "Cool." It was very nice but I got similar feelings with my MBA certificate. When I got that piece of paper, the delivery boy went up to San Francisco to pick it up for me. I was holding that piece of paper. I had one tear, and then I put it into my pouch and that was it. It is nice. The key word to everyone here is the process. Enjoy the journey.

At the end of the journey, at the end of a train journey, you expect a balloon to be there: horn blowing, people partying. Actually you should enjoy the process. The process of working with my peers, of working overnight in a garage until 4am or 5am. Or in the hot summer afternoon, in an inferno that reached 115 degrees in the garage. My first office was in my garage with ISDN Systems. I didn't have enough money, well, you have to safeguard your money. You shouldn't spend any more than necessary.

Family

Q: *You must come from a great gene pool, I mean someone in your family must have passed something onto you, do you think that is a factor?*

A: I don't know, I'm the black sheep of the family. My elder brother is a Ph.D. and works for IBM; he runs three computers at the same time on his desk, and runs a datacenter; and he is an IBM fellow kind of guy. My younger brother is a doctor of pharmacy. He is in a Laguna Niguel hospital. So they all have Ph.D.s. I'm a Ph.D. dropout, I didn't get mine, I am so ashamed, I should go kill myself. Hey, I'm Chinese, you know. You got to learn piano and violin, you got to get your Ph.D. And if Mommy knows you didn't do it, then you are the black sheep, and that was it.

Challenges

Q: *What are the biggest challenges you think you had to overcome from the university to now?*

A: Back in the early '80s, Chinese food was rare. Food is a sign of how popular and accepted a culture is. The same thing with the job in Dayton, Ohio; at lunch time they asked, "What do you want to eat?" I said "Chinese." They said, "Sorry, there is no Chinese restaurant." This was in Dayton, Ohio, in 1979. I said, "No, no, I can't live there like that."

Q: *Of what was that an indicator for you?*

A: It was an indicator of how well they accepted the Chinese culture and the population there.

Q: *I sometimes talk to Chinese women's groups and one of the questions I get is, "How do I get noticed as a Chinese woman? I definitely perceive a glass ceiling."*

A: That's the wrong thing to differentiate, to say, "I'm Chinese, I'm a woman, I'm that or this..." I think the world is flat as Friedman's book says. I think men and women are the same, we are the same, we are equal—more so than we believe. If one man and one woman both compete with a Ph.D. and the theses are all good, if you take the names of person A, person B, it doesn't matter if the person is male or female, black, white whatever color you are; it's the end result that counts.

If you can present an idea, a concept, a technical piece that excels, you win. I don't care who you are, you're Martian, I don't care. Bring me the end result; bring me something we can all use.

Success

Q: *How do you define success?*

A: I don't know. Success is only a comparative word. Where you came from, where you are today, where you are going; that defines your success. A Bronx kid, or someone from Brooklyn or somewhere else who gets out, goes to a good school, he excels today to become a multi-millionaire, a businessman; that's his way of measuring success. But, a Beverly Hills man who goes out and becomes a millionaire, is that a smaller success? Maybe the parents say, "This is not a success, it is shame on the family."

Q: *What about for you personally?*

A: Oh boy, how do I define myself? I don't think I am successful yet. I am still trying. If I can help the geniuses in the Valley start wonderful companies and I can help them to be more successful—then I think I have done my job. I have gravitated now to helping people versus doing it full time myself. I still work long hours, I didn't sleep till after midnight last night. I think my experience and the things I have done, those I can share with people. They are better utilized by sharing with people.

Q: *So your success would be helping other people to become successful?*

A: Yes, making sure their dreams come true, that their business plan is right, that it's written correctly, that they see the right VCs and I invest in them and help them out. Maybe I'll be their chairman or sit on the board as an advisor.

Silicon Valley as a Main Ingredient

Q: *Could you have done all this outside Silicon Valley?*

A: Not so easy, not so easy. The culture is very different in Silicon Valley as compared to elsewhere. I just want to let you know one thing. In 1976, I left Hong Kong to go to school in Salt Lake City, Utah. When I landed, I was walking fast like a man from Hong Kong; I was walking fast, talking fast. I tell you they were not used to me, "You're a freak, man, what are you doing? Stop being so fast."

Three and a half years later after I had come down to Silicon Valley, I was still talking fast but I had slowed down a lot already, still I was very fast. So I continued to slow myself down for the sake of the culture here. At last, I talk slower.

Q: *So this area is the right place to become something or someone?*

A: Yes, if you are a high energy person, you are a high achiever, and you have lots of energy as compared to the guy next door, you should absolutely be in Silicon Valley. There is no place I'd rather be than Silicon Valley, especially when you are in high tech.

If you are flipping hamburgers here, you better go somewhere else because the minimum pay here is $7.00 an hour or something like that; and $7.00 per hour is nothing here in the Valley. $7.00 can be really good in another less populated state.

Advice to Chinese

Q: *What advice would you give to Chinese either who live here or come here to work? What three things should they be doing so that they rise above the others?*

A: If you are into technology, maybe Chinese or Indian or even French, German or Brazilian, you should continue to do what you feel is right. You should go chase after your dream that you feel is right.

You should be making good with what you have. A good idea, develop that and help the world. You can "save the world," sure, but sometimes if you don't, you can at least make the world a better place to be. Maybe a faster speed router, maybe a better chip, maybe better software or a medical device to help people. You should chase after your dream and do it. Find people to help you, don't do it all by yourself. Especially the Chinese that I encounter, they think they can do everything. It's what I call the "King syndrome." One king on top, and many men under. There is no hierarchy, there is no delegation. It's a "Ma and Pa shop" that cannot scale.

An entrepreneur just came to me, he was a one man band, a one man army and he said, "I developed this, I invented it, I'm doing it." I said, "Who is your team"? "I don't have a team, I don't need a team." "What do you mean you don't need a team, what if you die tomorrow?" I have to invest in someone who has a team.

Iron Chef Silicon Valley

Q: *What do you do to relax?*

A: My way to relax is cooking. During SARS, I couldn't fly to China, so we started an "Iron Chef Silicon Valley Club." We just cater informally once in a while. We originally had a pot luck, but one day I couldn't bring anything, so I said, "Why don't I buy the ingredients and cook right in front of you guys?" They went crazy over it, and we started Iron Chef. I said, "Let's do Iron Chef Silicon Valley." And it really helps build relationships, you have to eat anyway. You cook up a storm right in front of your friends, and everyone chips in. "No, no this is the way to do the garlic, you don't need to slam on it, you need to cut on it." We have a ball.

Eric Buatois, Managing Partner, Sofinnova

Eric Buatois
Managing Director, Sofinnova
Country of Origin: France
Group: The VCs

> *"The leaders who are successful in a multicultural environment need to have soft skills that are stronger than the rational aspect of doing business."*

While Eric is known for his hard work, he also knows how to take time off. Before he started to work in Silicon Valley, he and his wife sailed the Caribbean for six months with their young daughter.

Q: *How would you describe what you are doing professionally today?*

A: I am a venture capitalist. The job of a venture capitalist is to identify new promising ideas, new promising entrepreneurs, and to participate in their projects, by obviously taking ownership in exchange for money. More importantly, we help them fine-tune their plan, find their first customer, and finalize the product definition. And we also help them recruit their management team.

Q: *How did your childhood experiences or your family upbringing influence your choice of career?*

A: I am not sure I can find the traces in my childhood, but I am lucky, I have always been very good in the sciences as well as in the humanities.

When I did the French baccalaureate I hesitated between sciences, which is the track for engineering, versus literature and philosophy.

This duality has played an important role in the development of my career. Every time I've been in engineering, I wanted to be in touch with people, and every time I was working more with people, I wanted to be in touch with science.

Education

Q: *You made a big leap between your baccalaureate and where you are now. Fill us in a little bit on your life. What motivated you to come here?*

A: I am a typical guy who went through the *Grandes Écoles* in France. I did my Master's Degree at the *École Nationale Superieure de Télécommunication*. Then I went to work for Texas Instruments, designing the LSI, big complex integrated circuits, big designs, big chips.

Designing the Heart of the Cell Phone

Immediately I was pretty lucky to be right in the entrepreneur spirit. I happened to work on a special chip called a digital signal processor, which is now the heart of the cell phone and is a core TI business. I started this business, a new initiative with different people who now have big responsibilities at TI.

It was a lot of fun and I still have a very close relationship with the people who worked with me at that time and who are now at the top of the company. I really enjoyed it.

But then there was a huge crisis in the mid eighties in the semiconductor sector and at that time, I was approached by a headhunter to join Hewlett-Packard. The company was in Grenoble, France. This was about a start-up within HP and I was one of the two guys who started this telecom business. I joined in '87 and in ten years, we brought this business from zero to four or five billion dollars.

So up to that time, I had done my science work at TI and now I went and worked on my business side at HP.

Q: *How did you make the jump from HP to where you are now?*

A: I was at HP at this time in France, and then I had the idea to create a joint venture with Ericsson, because at the time Ericsson was very successful selling mobile infrastructure.

We got this team of 50 or 60 engineers and I created this company, EHPT–Eriksson, Hewlett-Packard Telecom.

Q: *And how did you come to the United States?*

A: The board of the company was composed of half Eriksson and half the people from HP. Bernard Guidon who was working in the telecom business, was due to take another assignment at HP. At that time, he was in charge of the service business at HP, so he told me "I need someone to run the telecom business. Why don't you come to California and do it?" This is a typical Silicon Valley story because you meet, have dinner, and say yes.

Success

Q: *What does it mean for you to be successful?*

A: To be successful is to be in line with oneself. A lot of people define success as the way people measure you from the outside, so many people measure success by the house they have or the car they drive.

But for me, you are successful if your inner values and inner objectives are in line with how people perceive you. For me, being successful is doing a job I like, where I have a lot of freedom. Of course, you have to make money if you're going to be in venture capitalism.

I need a job that I like and I have passion in every day. I have always been a passionate guy and since I have been in the VC business, I never had a day where I didn't have some funny things happen to me. I have the kick to do something every day. I have freedom and great opportunities to work with the people I want to work with. For me that is a huge, fabulous opportunity. People I don't like, I don't work with. Sometimes, when you work in a big company, that's a problem.

Q: *Did your background being French give you any unique advantage?*

A: We are at an obvious disadvantage—the language. I think my generation has had the advantage of benefiting from a fabulous, public education. I still think the education system in France was outstanding. And the "unfair" advantage that I had was that I worked with a lot of people from a lot of different cultures and nationalities, and better yet, I still have that balance between science and humanities.

Challenges of Multicultural Leadership

Q: *What are the greatest challenges for multicultural leadership today?*

A: It's being exposed to multicultural leadership. I think my generation had it easier. I come from this multicultural world where everyone is learning what multiculture means. I was in a generation in the '80s where being international wasn't important, all it meant was you traveled.

Today, under pressure, with a lot of email and iChat and whatever, where everybody talks broken English, it's a bit dangerous. I know we believe we understand the other, but I am not sure we have time to understand.

Understanding Culture

Q: *What do you have to do to be the leader in this multicultural environment?*

A: In my mind it is still important to fully understand the people. I would argue to understand the people, you have to have lived abroad.

You only see yourself—your value set—when you are put into another world. If you stay in your own culture, you don't know what your own culture is. So for me, the most important thing is to have been abroad, where you have to have your habits, your culture, and acceptance by other people, it is then you know who you are. Through this adaptation process, you really understand what multicultural means.

I think number two is to be curious. If you are not curious, and you don't want to learn, it won't work. I worked in an environment where I had a very diverse team. I remember in one team, I had 11 different nationalities. You have to be genuine with the people because people sense that immediately.

The leaders who are successful in a multicultural environment need to have soft skills that are stronger than the rational aspect of doing business. People who are very top down, very analytical, I am not so sure that they are successful in a multicultural environment.

Leader Qualifications

Q: *What are three important things to keep in mind as a good leader?*

A: I think as a leader you have to realize that people always look up to you. You lead more by what you do than by what you say. For example, I know people are concerned how you make a presentation to the monthly preview team. But in practice, people judge you by what you do, how fast you decide, or don't decide. For me, that's very important.

The second important thing is for you to know what's happening in your organization. You defeat the point of leadership if you only get input from people only one level below you. You need to put your roots and antennas into whole the organization. That means you need to schmooze and mingle with all kinds of different people to really know what's happening.

A leader shouldn't be afraid to be unpopular. As a good leader, you always have to be more of a visionary. And typically you get your inspiration and articulate your vision by what's happening outside of the business of your company—for example, from your customers—and you have a vision showing the company how to get there.

Advice

Q: *What advice would you give French, Chinese or Indians who are either living here or coming here if they want to make a difference?*

A: You have to spend time to understand this country, especially for those coming from a small country, including the French. In Europe, the countries are pretty monolithic in their culture. I know there are differences between France and Germany and among the different regions within the countries, but we are still pretty much a homogenous structure as compared to over here in the U.S. Typically as a European coming here, you have this image of a unified American culture.

So when Frenchmen come here, they have to understand that here are a lot of subsets of cultures; my advice is to forget the American model, forget about the "American way." We need to spend time to understand that America is a combination of subcultures, or almost sub-countries, there are big differences depending on which part of the U.S. you look at. So that's really my big advice.

I would add and remind them that this is a country of immigrants and the immigrants are successful in this country if they integrate by doing things in a certain way. If you come here not to integrate, that's not good, because that is the DNA of this country. You come and you integrate. You have a lot of personal freedom but you do need to adapt to the local culture.

We live in a very creative area, but people have to realize that California is not the U.S. California is a subculture and is probably becoming one of the richest subcultures in diversity in the various ways of doing things.

I would advise people to do the same when they look at China and India, perhaps more so when they go to India. In India, they have 24 different states; you have to remind people that this country has all the different variations of the countries in Europe. So when you move from one Indian state to the next one, it's like moving from Germany to Italy, therefore people need to be very clear about that when they do business in places like India.

Chapter

3 The Engineer(s)

The original story of Silicon Valley is the story of engineers. In 1939, two engineering graduates from Stanford University tinkered in their garage in Palo Alto and Hewlett-Packard was born. In later years, engineers from around the world have found a home in Silicon Valley to turn their ideas into world-beating products. One of them has succeeded over and over again and is inspired to continue. Andy Bechtolsheim tells the story of the Engineers.

Andy Bechtolsheim, Co-Founder, Sun Microsystems

> *"My passion in life is to build better products."*

Andy Bechtolsheim
Co-Founder, Sun Microsystems
Country of Origin: Germany
Group: The Engineer(s)

Andy Bechtolsheim talked with me for a good 45 minutes in a beautiful Sun Microsystems building in Menlo Park. Since rejoining Sun, he continues to work on innovative products.

My Career

I am a computer architect by training. In my first life at Sun, I spent most of my career designing Sun's workstation computers. At Cisco, I spent most of my time managing a good size engineering team. Coming back to Sun, I am now spending most of my time on defining new products and meeting with customers. Thus over the years I have done both engineering and management functions, as well as having been CEO and President of several startup companies.

The common thread in my career is that I truly enjoy building better products, independent of whether I am in a startup company or in a large public company. I love to apply my knowledge of technology to solve customer problems in new and better ways.

Family Background

I grew up on a farm in Bavaria, Germany. My dad was a schoolteacher and my mother was a homemaker. I have two brothers. One is a musician and the other a psychologist. I'm the only one in my family who had an interest in engineering or business.

As early as I remember I was always interested in how things worked. I started building my first radio when I was six years old. I learned how to make solder connections and still remember the smell of the solder iron, which smelled like magic to me.

High School Years

At the time I grew up—I was in high school in the late '60s, early '70s—there were no computers available to students. There were no computer classes and there was no other way to get access to computers. I was able to get one of the first Intel 8080 CPUs in Germany in 1973, and I built a computer system around it and to my surprise everything just worked.

I remember learning all the binary machine codes and typing in the program with digital switches into the memory of this computer I built.

So I learned about computers by building a computer. Until I came to the United States, I had no formal training of any type in computer design or programming. It is actually something that is very hard to learn from a book or attending lectures. You learn it by doing. My general experience in life is that most of what I learned was learned by doing.

Education

The arrival of the first microcomputers in the early '70s started a very exciting time in the computer field. In 1975, I enrolled at the Technische University in Munich hoping to learn more about computer designs, but in one of the biggest disappointments in my life at the time, there were no specialized classes for computer design, and all the course work had to do with applied physics and how to build high voltage towers and electrical motors. I was completely bored at the university and I started to worry I would miss the entire microcomputer revolution. I figured if anybody knew how to build computers, it would be in the United States. So I applied for a Fulbright scholarship to come to the U.S., and luckily I got it.

Coming to the United States

When I came to the U.S., it was a completely different experience. I spent two years at Carnegie Mellon University in Pittsburgh, which has an outstanding Computer Science department and they received a lot of government funding to build next generation computer systems. It was a deep immersion experience. Basically in the two years I was there, I would wake up in the morning at 7:00, eat breakfast at the cafeteria, show up at the Computer Science building, and go home at midnight. Except for holiday breaks, I never left the campus.

I got my Master's Degree in 1976 for a project on how to build the network interface for a cluster computer built out of microprocessors, which of all things is what I am still working on today, 30 years later.

Coming to Silicon Valley

Even though I enjoyed my multiprocessor project at Carnegie Mellon, I always wanted to come to Silicon Valley in California since this was the birthplace of the microprocessor and clearly where the future of computers was happening. In 1977, I had a summer job lined up with Intel Corporation and I drove my car cross country, but just as I arrived in Silicon Valley, the person who had offered me this job was transferred to Intel's new facility in Oregon. I could have followed him to Oregon, but I really wanted to be here in Silicon Valley.

So I was here and had nothing to do. I stayed with a friend of mine who was a computer operator at Stanford and he showed me around. It was there I saw a job listing to do some CAD (computer-aided design) programming. I knew something about CAD so I applied and started work in a summer job at Stanford.

At the end of the summer, the professor I worked with suggested that I should just transfer to Stanford, and I did. So I never actually applied to come to Stanford, I just arrived one day and did not leave until I started Sun five years later.

Needless to say Stanford is a wonderful place, the campus, the weather, and the vicinity to Silicon Valley. The Stanford Computer Science department also had funding from DARPA, the Defense Advanced Research Project Agency, and in 1979, we proposed to them to build a workstation computer such that every student and researcher would have their own computer with built-in interactive graphics and networking.

This was a very interesting project and it took me less than a year to put the build the first prototype.

Breaking into Business

I built about 20 prototypes at Stanford. As word leaked out, suddenly a lot of people were interested in this and of all things, wanted to buy one.

At that point it was clear that something had to change since Stanford University, a non-profit educational institution, was not in the business of making computers. We had a meeting, and I said I would start a company to get these things made.

At that time I met Vinod Khosla whose best friend was Scott McNealy, and the three of us very quickly wrote a business plan to set this up as a manufacturing company, and we immediately got funding. Bill Joy, Sun's fourth founder, joined a few weeks later from Berkeley, where he was leading the development of the BSD Berkeley UNIX software distribution, which was the operating system most widely used by researchers at the time.

The new company was called Sun Microsystems, named after the Stanford University Network project I worked on at Stanford. The company took off very quickly. Just four years after we were founded, we were a public company; and in the fifth year, Sun had sales of over $1 billion. It was one of the fastest growing startup companies in the history of computers.

Background as a Foreigner

Obviously I am a foreigner. Vinod Khosla is a foreigner. Two out of the four founders of Sun Microsystems were foreigners.

If I look at the average student population in Electrical Engineering or Computer Science at Stanford, I think it's pretty much the same ratio. Roughly half of them if not more are foreigners. Many of these students have gone on to start or build important new businesses, so the contributions of all these foreign students to the American economy cannot be understated.

I don't think that being a foreigner made much difference to my success in Silicon Valley. I was not treated differently from anyone else because I was a foreigner. I found Silicon Valley to be about as open-minded to a foreigner coming here as I could imagine.

Certainly foreigners are treated very differently in other parts of the world—where you stick out as a sore thumb if you are from a different county. In Silicon Valley there are so many foreigners that it is basically a multicultural society. People understand that this is an egalitarian work environment, and an open-minded country and society.

This is a huge benefit over countries where, if you are not the right nationality, you don't have the opportunity to be the manager or progress in your career. There is definitely no class system here. Individual contribution and individual skill and hard work is really what makes people's careers here.

One of the bizarre things about the U.S. immigration policy is that there are fewer visas available today for foreign engineers to come and stay in this country than in previous years, so the advantage that the U.S. enjoyed in terms of all this talent that wants to come here is being eroded; plus, there are new opportunities for the same talent in China and India, so the competition is actually increasing.

In my experience, the foreign engineers who come to this country work extra hard to be able to stay here and to take advantage of the opportunities that exist here. This behavior should be encouraged and rewarded, not inhibited.

Many high-tech companies in Silicon Valley were started by foreigners and have hired many foreign engineers. Thus a lot of the success of Silicon Valley is due to foreign nationals that have come here to live.

Overcoming Obstacles

I always had a very intense desire to do exactly what I wanted to do, both in coming to this country and starting the companies that I did. This is still true for me today. My passion in life, if you will, is to build better products. And while a lot of people think I am calm on the outside, I am actually very competitive internally.

It is an intellectual chess game. You need to find better solutions to problems. You get to make so many moves and you have to understand your opponents' moves and strategies and what they think they are going to do. In order to win the game, you need to make smarter moves than your opponent.

Benefits of Silicon Valley

The same way that Hollywood is the headquarters for making movies, Silicon Valley is the epicenter for high tech. All the outsourcing doesn't change that. Of course movies are also being made in New Zealand and Canada and many other places, but the core expertise on how to make a great movie still is in Hollywood.

Starting a high-tech company outside Silicon Valley is much more difficult. In my own case, I could have not started Sun or any of the other companies that I was involved with outside of Silicon Valley. It would have been too difficult.

I have met with several German start-ups that keep wondering what they could do to grow faster. My usual advice for them is to come to Silicon Valley. The U.S. market is much larger; and you have more credibility as an American startup than as a German one even you sell in Germany.

The environment of Silicon Valley is simply the most fertile one you can imagine. If a new startup does not succeed here, it probably was not a good idea.

There are so many smart people here that innovation has become a way of life. The intellectual stimulation one gets in this kind of environment is unbelievable. I feel much younger as a person in my heart and mind than I am in years. The opportunity to exchange new ideas is higher here than anywhere else.

In some cases I also had a chance to invest in startup companies and work with the entrepreneurs in these companies. It is a pleasure to see people working really hard in pursuit of their business goals. These entrepreneurs work 60 to 80 hours a week to reach their goals and never take a vacation. Those are the kind of people I like to work with.

Measuring Success

Measuring success is a very personal thing. Certainly one achieves success by having goals, and I have always done that in my life. If you don't set yourself clear goals, you are highly unlikely to get there.

However, the deeper meaning of success is to find personal satisfaction in what you do. The reward is the journey, as the saying goes. The journey can take many years, whereas achieving the goal is just a fleeting moment.

I always focus on goals where I can truly make a difference. I need to feel that I can make a real contribution since each goal tends to involve a lot of hard work.

I do see other people who are also very energetic, but if they pursue the wrong goals, it doesn't help them. They can work as hard as they want, but unless the work results in a great product or market success, they are wasting their time.

Leadership

As a leader you have to be able to articulate clearly why we are going to do this, what's important about it, what's the purpose, who are the customers and so on. People follow you based on matching the future reality, but you're typically two years out. So you need to be able to connect the present to the future. You have to explain it to people so they are willing to take the steps required to get there.

There is this thing called the *horizon effect*. If you cannot see over the horizon, you never go there. This is true for general life. People tend to only pursue goals that they believe they can achieve, because if you can't get there, why start.

Advice to Other Foreigners

Some people come here to study and then they return home. That is a very different scenario than coming here with the intention to live and work here.

Until a few years ago, it was obvious this was the place to come if you wanted to have a career in high tech. There was no question about it. Recently, it has become more difficult to come here as a foreigner. There are not as many visas as there should be, and there are also more good opportunities at home.

Few Regrets

I have very few regrets in my life. I always did what I wanted to do. I never thought of work as work, but as a means to achieve my goals. For many people, work is something they have to do to earn a living. To me, work is what I do because I am interested in doing it. The fascinating opportunity in high tech is to shape the future with better products. This has been my goal in all my life.

Chapter

4 The Academic Businessmen

Academic institutions have played a crucial role in the Valley's transformation. Stanford University, founded in 1891, was the alma mater of Bill Hewlett and Dave Packard. Stanford gave its name to Sun Microsystems (originally the Stanford University Network). Other well-known companies that began as Stanford start-ups include SGI, Yahoo!, Cisco, Collagen, Varian and, most noticeably, Google.[8]

Stanford University, however, is not the only influential school in Silicon Valley. Other institutions such as San Jose State University and Santa Clara University play a crucial role as well other universities in the U.S., among them MIT and Carnegie Mellon. Many foreign professionals first come to the U.S. on a student visa. Others are already trained in the top schools of their countries (Les Grandes Écoles of France, The IITs of India) and come here for graduate studies and their Ph.D. degrees. Hear what Rajesh Gupta and Arno Penzias have to say:

---

8. Gibbons, J., "The Role of Stanford University," in Lee, C.M. et al., The Silicon Valley Edge: A Habitat for Innovation and Entrepreneurship, Stanford University Press, 2000, 203.

- Rajesh Gupta, Professor, Computer Science, UC San Diego
- Arno Penzias, Venture Partner, New Enterprises Associates, (Nobel Prize, 1978)

Rajesh Gupta, Professor, Computer Science, UC San Diego

Rajesh Gupta
Professor, Computer Science, UC San Diego
Country of Origin: India
Group: The Academic Entrepreneur

> *"As a multicultural society, America is perhaps unparalleled in human history: it has a lot to offer by way of education on how to live and work among totally different peoples and create an environment in which everyone is successful to their fullest."*

Rajesh Gupta teaches at UC San Diego. I connected with him while he was on a sabbatical visit to the Bay Area and later on his way to École Polytechnique in Lausanne, Switzerland.

Q: *How would you describe what you are doing professionally today?*

A: I am on a sabbatical leave from UC San Diego, where I teach Computer Science. We have an active research group in the Microelectronics Embedded Systems Laboratory at UC San Diego. We are also engaged in several interdisciplinary projects as a part of the California Institute for Telecommunications and Information Technology.

Q: *Here in the Bay Area, I understand you also interact with companies and venture capitalists, what do you do with the VCs?*

A: Truthfully, I am learning more from the VCs than perhaps the other way around. Yet, my role as a consulting professor is to examine the evolving technology and advise the executives in residence or industry leaders regarding strengths and weaknesses, and what they can expect from future advancements in technologies related to semiconductors and computing systems transitioning from research institutions—also what the barriers to their adoption in the marketplace will be.

Childhood Influences

Q: *How did your childhood experiences and/or your family influence your choice of career?*

A: When I was in elementary school, the first wave of satellites was launched. There was a lot of news about that. So, I wanted to be a "space scientist" at ISRO, the Indian equivalent of NASA. My teacher told me that you have to be smart and work very hard to make it to ISRO. As they say, a moment of imagination can lead to a lifetime of learning. It is quite true. I did not end in space research, but I did study hard.

Q: *What or who do you think motivated you to be who you are today?*

A: I had this sense from early childhood that to be successful in life, one must do something that will outlast one's lifetime and leave an impact for the future. I don't exactly know where this value came from; it could have been from something I picked up from my parents or even from any of the religious stories that we heard growing up. Anyhow, for some reason, there was a measure of success that subconsciously drove major life decisions. It helped that the society I grew up in valued higher education and often held up people who had done well in education as role models, be it as engineers, doctors or in administrative service. So, getting a good education became a necessary path in my mind to be successful in life.

Coming to the U.S.

Q: *How did you get to the United States?*

A: I did my undergraduate studies at IIT Kanpur. The IITs have now gained a well-deserved recognition in the U.S. IITs provided an extraordinarily rich environment for students to learn and grow. But more importantly, it was also a great institution socially.

Once a student made it through the extraordinarily tough and competitive examination well enough to be admitted at any of the five IITs (now seven), there was no other barrier to a good education. Practically no tuition, and a required on-campus living experience that served as a great leveler for students coming from all socio-economic backgrounds. I say "living experience," since more than housing, it defined all aspects of life as a shared experience: from meals to watching movies and many of the extra-curricular clubs in the residential halls. Classes were small, the entire engineering batch in a year was about 250-300 students spread across all the departments. So, one got to know the batch mates really well. After IIT, the standard path to higher education then led through U.S. universities. I came to Berkeley since it offered a full scholarship through a fellowship.

Challenges and Directions

Q: *Did you ever have crossroads that you came to and your life would have been totally different if you had made another choice?*

A: Leaving Berkeley with an M.S. instead of a Ph.D. for a job at Intel was a turning point. I had not planned on that. However, my time at Berkeley was a difficult time health-wise: a couple of surgeries, loss of hearing in one ear, concerns about a tumor recurring in the middle ear, etc. It was a mixed experience, but in the end it was the right choice: Intel turned out to be a great learning experience. I just loved being there. Three years later, the transition from Intel to Stanford was also an important one, but perhaps not as critical to personal growth. Intel was rewarding, and perhaps could have been a totally different path had I stayed there, compared to the path to academics starting with the Ph.D. at Stanford.

Q: *Do you regret that?*

A: No, I don't. My goal was to be a researcher, and I couldn't be one without a doctorate. I feel fortunate that it turned out well, and I love being an academic.

Success

Q: *What does it mean to be successful today?*

A: You make an impact for the better. An impact may be how others think about something, do things, or even their outlook towards life in general. Success measures have to be defined in relation to the society we live in, or the community we are a part of.

Leadership Today

Q: *What are the greatest challenges for multicultural leadership today?*

A: Leadership challenges are the same, the multicultural environment just adds a dynamic that requires reading across cultural languages to make sound judgments. To be a good leader, one has to be a good team player first, and then find ways to make the team outperform what it thinks it can do.

Advice

Q: *What advice would you give Indians who are either living here or coming to work?*

A: As a multicultural society, America is perhaps unparalleled in human history: it has a lot to offer by way of education on how to live and work among totally different peoples and create an environment in which everyone is successful to their fullest. But these benefits require taking the time to understand and appreciate the American work ethics and values. For those of us who go through the educational system here, this task of acclimatization is somewhat easier than for those who hit the workplace directly. But all of us have to be aware of the unique nature of the society, and especially Silicon Valley, that brings out the best in all of us.

Arno Penzias, Venture Partner, New Enterprises Associates (Nobel Prize, 1978)

Arno Penzias
Venture Partner, New Enterprise Associates
Country of Origin: Germany
Group: The Academic Entrepreneurs

> *"Everyone says that Silicon Valley is youth oriented – I don't believe it. Silicon Valley is age agnostic."*

Arno Penzias talked to me on the phone. He has a dynamic personality and spent time helping me understand his background and also kindly answered my burning question, "What did it feel like winning a Nobel Prize?"

Q: *Tell me what you are doing today.*

A: I work with a venture capital firm focusing mostly on alternative energy and a variety of other technologies.

Childhood Influences

Q: *How did your childhood and your family influence you to be where you are today?*

A: The main thing which I share with a whole generation of refugees, is coming out of Germany from a certain German culture, and getting out and moving to another place where you have very few upward obstacles, very little to lose, and no choice of moving anywhere but forward.

Q: *Did you move directly from Germany to the United States?*

A: My father and I came from Germany in late 1938. My father had Polish citizenship and we were deported to the Polish border. We had Polish passports, so what happened was the Germans "played chicken" with the Poles and tried to get rid of all their Jews across the border.

Fortunately, because we came out of Munich and it was after the end of the October deadline where the Polish passports were no longer valid, we got to Poland, but we didn't end up in the field where many people died of exposure. We were allowed back into Germany. My father continued working with and helping the Dachau survivors. In those days people got out of Dachau and were sent by suburban train back to Munich.

He and some of the other young members of the Jewish community would be up every night meeting the trains from Dachau, carrying off what was left of the people and burying bodies. So he knew we wanted to get out. After Kristallnacht, (November 9th, 1938) we moved around a little bit. My father, because of Kristallnacht, predicted we would have a Kindertransport Program. I was put into that together with my younger brother. (Children were sent to London for safekeeping.)

Q: *And what happened to your parents?*

A: Both my parents were lucky enough to get out before the war started, within weeks. And, it ended up that we came to the United States in December of 1939. I went to a New York City school and the rest was easy.

Q: *How did your parents influence you in terms of culture and striving to go forward or maybe a love of business, or a love of science?*

A: My father barely finished high school. But he had great respect for chemistry. We always talked about the fact that kids were expected to go to college and we were quite poor.

Anyhow, I didn't expect to be rich, but I did not want to be poor. I figured science would be a way to begin. City College was free, so I went there. I did three years in the Army, five years at Columbia University, went to Bell Labs, and then I retired and here I am.

Bell Labs

I got the job running a research organization about three weeks before the AT&T Justice Department deal went into action in late 1981. I was left then with 80 percent of my funding going out the other side.

So at that point, I gave up whatever fundamental research I was doing and worked to make the big research valuable to the company and to the owners. And after going to the other side, I wanted to do something different; I didn't want to stay there until the age of 65. It was actually in the middle of 1995, when I was 62 years old, that I told them I was quitting. I moved out to California, there they made me chief scientist of what then became Lucent Technologies.

The VC Track

I set a goal and I moved out here. I wanted to learn by doing, I wanted to learn about Silicon Valley. I didn't want to go to meetings and certainly not read the trade rags of what other people think.

I tend to look at things myself. I rarely stop talking but I do listen. I want to find out what is really going on. So what I did was, I started attending presentations at various VC firms.

Q: *What was your goal to listen at these presentations, for what?*

A: I was listening in order to become familiar with what was going on, but at the same time, I was doing what I do best: asking questions, actually questions that had implied suggestions.

A lot of VCs were asking questions but most of the time the VCs couldn't grasp what they were listening to. So I helped them understand, and I have been a venture partner ever since.

Obstacles? Success?

Q: *What were your greatest obstacles and successes in your career?*

A: Obstacles? I have had a lot of different ones. One of the obstacles was getting on the wrong side of people for lots of different reasons—some my fault, some theirs. The biggest obstacles have been a yin and yang.

When I look at anything, I almost always look at things in another way. One day the CEO of AT&T met my wife in a meeting and she said, "You might know my husband."

He said, "Yes. Of course I know him. Whenever we talk about anything, he always sees things in a different way." It was enough to get me promoted to the head of the research organization, but it was the kind of thing that would keep me from being the president of Bell Labs.

I think my greatest success is seeing things in ways other people haven't seen them. And, I think, that has also been the source of my biggest problems.

Q: *But isn't seeing things in a unique way appreciated in Silicon Valley?*

A: It's more appreciated in Silicon Valley, but it was also appreciated at Bell Labs by other researchers. What I like about Silicon Valley is that it is very results-oriented. The discussions are nowhere near as interesting as on the East Coast, let alone the ones in Europe, because here, they're very results-oriented.

Everyone says that Silicon Valley is youth oriented—I don't believe it. Silicon Valley is age agnostic.

Good Leadership Skills

Q: *What are the things that are really important to keep in mind to be a good leader?*

A: I ran a $300 million a year business—Bell Labs Research—with over a thousand people, most of them prima donnas, and with a management that had very little clue about what I was doing. I certainly was doing leadership there.

One of the important things is listening; even though I talk a lot, I do watch out for what people are thinking. I look at how they're reacting. I think that the other important thing about leadership is being curious and interested and having an open mind.

Nobel Prize 1978

Q: *What was it like winning the Nobel Prize?*

A: In my case, I was working the whole time. As you might expect, I felt a little unworthy and I questioned whether I deserved this. Am I really that smart? I certainly felt a little strange. I didn't want to be measured on whether I deserved it or not. The only question I wanted to answer was, "Did I put that prize to good use or not?"

Together with Robert Woodrow Wilson, Penzias won the 1978 Nobel Prize in Physics for their work on what was later identified as the cosmic microwave background radiation (CMB), the radio remnant of the Big Bang. This allowed astronomers to confirm the Big Bang theory, and to correct many of their previous assumptions about it.

While I was in Stockholm, I gave interviews to every single German television station and told my childhood story. And, it felt great when I went back in 2001 for the 50th Anniversary and I could now say "Nobel Prize winner" without stammering.

One of the biggest honors that I had was that I was the second person Andre Sakharov met with when he came to the United States. He came here to the U.S. to see the doctors and on the second day, he came to see me because he wanted to talk about the SDI initiatives; and so I got a phone call and went to his stepdaughter's apartment and talked to him for hours. It was certainly a reward for the things I had managed to do up to this point about the people being repressed in the Soviet Union up to the 1980s.

Advice for Foreign-Born Entrepreneurs

Q: *What advice would you give foreign-born entrepreneurs who come to Silicon Valley or the United States who want to do well?*

A: It really depends on the culture they come from. I would say, "Become aware of your own cultural differences and how they are different from those in the United States." This is very hard for some people. You have to become really aware of these differences and if you're not aware of them, you're not going to be able to work well in this society. You have to look at yourself and understand your own culture to be able to understand others. Mix up the picture, don't stay with what you are most comfortable with.

Chapter

5 The Start-Up Wizards

If the wealth of nations were generated by established firms, the British would still be the world's largest producers, and East Coast steel would out-rank silicon chips in value. Change is the engine of economic growth. Silicon Valley has experienced many distinct periods when wealth generated from previously unknown technology. Start-ups in chip design were hot in the 1970s. The Internet start-ups grew out of nowhere in the late 1990s and search engine companies like Google or social networking firms such as Facebook or LinkedIn are changing the environment in the 2000s.

The unique advantage of start-ups is that they are able to move rapidly to capitalize on disruptive innovation, which established companies either don't see or won't tackle for fear of cannibalizing their existing product lines.[9]

Being involved in a start-up is the quintessential route to riches in Silicon Valley. People who start new companies often have a revolutionary

---

9. Gibbons, J., "The Role of Stanford University," in Lee, C.M. et al., The Silicon Valley Edge: A Habitat for Innovation and Entrepreneurship, Stanford University Press, 2000, 203.

attitude and want to change the world with their brilliant ideas. They embrace risk. Some achieve astronomical rewards. These people are the pure form of immigrant entrepreneur. Often starting with nothing more than an idea sketched on the back of a napkin and an insane desire to succeed: they seize every opportunity this region has to offer. And some come back again and again realizing new ideas in bursts of creativity. Listen to the stories of the Start-Up Wizards:

- Raj Singh, CEO and Founder, Sonoa Systems
- Suhas Patil, CEO, Cradle Technologies and Chairman of Digite and Arzoo, (Chairman Emeritus, Cirrus Logic)
- Wu Fu Chen, Founding Partner of Genesis Campus, Acorn Campus
- Dina Bitton, VP, SAP
- Samba Murthy, Founder and COO, Xambala

Raj Singh, CEO and Founder, Sonoa Systems

Raj Singh
CEO and Founder, Sonoa Systems
Country of Origin: India
Group: The Start-Up Wizards

> *"Success is like an antioxidant. It doesn't make any difference in life, except that you feel healthy."*

Samba Murthy connected Raj Singh and me. Raj has not only created seven start-ups, he is also a published author and successful film producer.

Current Status

Q: *Raj, how would you describe what you are doing professionally today?*

A: Well, I am managing a start-up which I started about 2-l/2 years ago, based on an idea which I had about three years ago. This company, Sonoa, is building an innovative product for data centers in order to enable real-time responses for Web services.

Childhood Influences

Q: *How did your childhood experiences and your family prepare you or influence you to where you are today?*

A: My family is agriculture-based, they are farmers in rural India and have been working with their own hands, tilling the land and selling the crops. What I learned from them is dedicated, hard work, that's all.

Q: *But then you must have gone to the university?*

A: Yes, I went to college in Meerut City. I did begin high school in the village, then for 11th and 12th grades I studied in Meerut City. Then I went to an engineering college in Roorkee, which is now an IIT and is now known as Roorkee University.

Early Career Choices

Q: *What did you do after IIT and how did you get to the United States?*

A: After IIT, I joined the Indian Navy for a while. When I left, I did a little business—Jay Electronics in Meerut City, India—and then went to IIT Delhi to do a Master's in Applied Mathematics. Then I worked for the

TATA Institute of Fundamental Research in Bombay, a research institute in Computer Science.

I then got a job in a start-up company, Alpha Electro, in Delhi, so I went to Delhi but the company closed after three years. After that, I went to Abu Dhabi, in the Middle East, to a telecom corporation, Emirtel Communications. After Abu Dhabi, I went to train in a government deputation job in Libya for three years where I was the Indian expert working in an electricity corporation in Libya.

Then I came to the U.S. when I was 33, because I thought there were more opportunities here and I went to school in Minneapolis to get my Master's Degree in Computer Science at the University of Minnesota.

Company Travel Bug

I went to join Control Data Corporation for three months, which was a job I didn't like, so I left and joined National Semiconductor, here in California, where I worked for nine months.

After that, I joined Trilogy Systems, a one-year-old start-up by Gene Amdahl, where I worked for three years until the company closed after going public. Later on I joined another start-up, Cirrus Logic in Milpitas. I worked for Dr. Suhas Patil [another Start-Up Wizard] the founder and VP of Technology, as a software engineer for two years. And then I joined another start-up, Nexgen Microsystems which was started by another Indian, Thampy Thomas. I introduced Atiq Reza to the company who joined them as VP of Engineering and later became its CEO.

Q: *You not only have the travel bug, you have the company travel bug too!*

A: I worked at Nexgen for six years, and while working, I wrote the book, *Digital Design and Synthesis with Verilog HDL*, published and sold by me, as no publisher would pick it. The book sold very well for ten years.

Based on that book, I started a company called InterHDL, to develop tools for chip design. I worked there for two years; and then I started another company, Advanced Corporation.

Q: *So what happened to the first corporation?*

A: I left it with my partner Eli Sternheim, It was sold to Avant! Corporation. In the meantime, I had done Advanced Corporation, which was developing intellectual property for communication and for Java microprocessors.

We developed a tiny version of a Java processor to accelerate Java (Java is a language by Sun Microsystems) and also communications property in ATMs. We licensed the technology to Adaptec, National, Cypress Semiconductor and IDT, and they developed chips based on that technology for ATMs.

I ran that company for about two years. And then I took out the communications IP and got it funded by Vinod Khosla, [at that time] a General Partner at Kleiner Perkins Caufield & Byers.

I left the Java company behind and moved to Fiberlane. Advanced with Java technology was later sold to Noise Cancellation Technology on the East Coast.

I did that company in Petaluma, Vancouver and Mountain View, three locations. Then a year later it was split into two companies: they became Cerent and Siara. Cerent was sold to Cisco and Siara was sold to Redback. A group of people who didn't go to either started Cyras, and I helped those people organize to start their own company. After I left Cerent, I started another company, Stratum One Communications. It got funding from VCs and Cisco, it developed a chip for telecom and was later sold to Cisco, too.

Simultaneously with Stratum One, I started a venture capital firm, Redwood Ventures, together with Raj Parekh from Sun; he used to work with Andy [Bechtolsheim], and then came to Comstellar together with Sanjiv Ahuja from the East Coast. Sanjiv Ahuja right now is the CEO of Orange, over in London, England [Sanjiv has since left that position].

Source of Ideas

Q: *How do you get these ideas? Do you have them at night, as in, "We should try this?"*

A: They don't come by night; you brainstorm with people and keep refining them. You talk to customers, you have some idea and then you see if that clicks with customers. I can't take credit for all that myself. I have always had a technology partner who would define the product while I would lead the business.

Making Movies

Q: *What did you do next?*

A: Then I quit and because I was very much interested in creativity, I got involved in the various aspects of movie making. So for four or five years, I worked with a few entrepreneurs in Hollywood who were coming out of film schools and I funded them to make movies.

Q: *Did you actually go to Los Angeles and work there?*

A: I used to go there off and on. I did spend time on the production floor for almost 80 percent of the duration to learn production and direction. I did everything in the filming from A-Z, including the distribution and film festivals; we went to several Film Festivals—such as Montreal, Toronto, Sundance and Manchester.

Singh executive produced (with: Richard Gere, Jeremy Thomas, Danny Reiner, Digvijay Singh and Somnath Sen) the films *Dreaming Lhasa* (2005), *The Great New Wonderful* (2005), *Leela* (2002), and *Mata* (2001)

Back to High Tech

After a while, I was getting a little bit out of touch with technology, so I met up with a couple of people who wanted to do something. We sat together and we started a company called Xambala, building the XML processor.

Then I thought of building a system by myself, and so I started Sonoa—I was also getting a bit bored at home.

Q: *So this will probably continue on, right?*

A: Yeah, that's how my life is; I'm thinking I should maybe move to India, there's a lot of action there. I visited Israel in 2000 to see what was happening there, and then I got a government invitation to visit China, in 2000. But now I am thinking of moving to India as I have gone there a few times to oversee Sonoa's India office. Interestingly, Sonoa is developing a state-of- the-art product out of India for the U.S. market.

Success Factors

Q: *What does it mean to you to be successful?*

A: Success means to have a good feeling, it means feeling good about yourself. I feel elated, and it grounds you too. Those five good minutes of elation. It's very healthy and boosts your immune system. Success is like an anti-oxidant. It doesn't make any difference in life, except that you feel healthy.

Silicon Valley's Continued Importance

Q: *Silicon Valley helped you a lot in that sense?*

A: Yes, it's is very fertile for these things, it already has the ecosystem that works for you. It has VCs and you have other people with similar thinking.

Q: *Do you think you could have done as well outside Silicon Valley?*

A: We don't know. I did one company in India by myself, which I had to close because our shipment was lost by the Indian Railways, and the second one that closed was started by someone else. It was gone because the government of India didn't want to give us the license to manufacture a minicomputer in the private sector.

Being Indian

Q: *Do you think your background as an Indian has given you advantages?*

A: I don't think so. When I came over here, I had a little disadvantage; I had worked for 12 years before coming here. When I negotiated my salary for my first job in the U.S., I was only offered a salary as if I had just graduated. They would not value my prior experience of 12 years in India and Libya. I said to them, "You know, give me a raise for the experience I already have, don't give me a base salary as if I were a fresh graduate." But at that time they said, "Well, we don't know what happens in India, so we cannot properly assess you."

Leadership Skills

Q:. *What is important in being a good multicultural leader today?*

A: A good leader is probably one who doesn't think he is a leader. The moment you think you are a leader, you start giving it a shape. So I think people like something that is natural in leaders. Whatever you have, leaders see it in the raw form, they are excited about it. What people like about me is probably I'm very passionate, and they see me the way I am, and I'm non-threatening to people.

A Disciplined Life

Q: *Last question, what do you do in your spare time?*

A: I do yoga every other day and I try (though not easily) to maintain a disciplined life.

Suhas Patil, CEO, Cradle Technologies and Chairman of Digite and Arzoo

Suhas Patil
CEO, Cradle Technologies, Chairman of Digite and Arzoo
(Chairman Emeritus, Cirrus Logic)
Country of Origin: India
Group: The Start-Up Wizards

> *"Success has been for me, on one side, professional success; it is to be able to follow a dream that otherwise would have been impossible; it is being able to achieve, this is life self-actuation, self-satisfaction. The second one is to be able to make a difference, to have an impact."*

Suhas was generous with his time, telling me stories about his family life in the small towns of India. He is a fabulous photographer who shared with me some of the beautiful pictures he has taken.

Q: *What are you doing professionally today?*

A: I am on boards of companies including Cirrus Logic [of which he was the founder] where I am Chairman Emeritus. I am working with younger companies as an angel investor where I am building companies of tomorrow. I select a few in which I get involved deeply.

I am also helping my wife who started *Fusion Fashion* magazine and a media company. Here the roles are reversed, she is the entrepreneur and I am the supportive husband.

Early Beginnings and Influences

Q: *What path did you follow to get to where you are today? What influences did you have from home?*

A: My early influences go back to where I was born in India. I was born in a town called Jamshedpur, about 170 miles west of Calcutta. This was a town established by its founder, Jamsetji Tata, to start the first steel plant.

The Tata steel plant's beginning happened about 50-60 years before I was born, and it was very evident growing up as a child, that there had been nothing but jungle before. And here was a person, Jamsetji Tata, who was not even from the area—he was from Bombay—he came scouting for iron ore; he had this vision to build a steel plant in India. His entrepreneurial story was folklore in the town. In those days, when you built a factory like that, you had to do everything including building the town, school and the hospital.

They built a small dam for water, the roads, the school, the housing—they ran the town because there was nothing there initially and later on, the towns ran themselves. The influence of that was: things can be done.

The next big influence was my father with his background in engineering, and the attitude of my mother. My father was the oldest in his family, and I was the oldest in mine.

Upward Mobility

Having gone to university, my father was invited to join Tata Steel. But, while he was a metallurgist at work, he decided he could do a radio repair business at home. Because of the radio business, my father had tools—a hacksaw, chisel, hammer, electric meters and the like and he showed me how to use them. So I found I could do metal work, just for the fun of it. This gave me dexterity and a confidence in building things.

As a teenager I discovered technical books and started learning "how to do" things, and I became quite capable in repairing mechanical, electronic things.

I got into IIT Kharagpur without any problem, and there I chose Electronics. We got a strong undergraduate training, very comparable to a U.S. education. That then gave me an opportunity and aspiration to think that I might like to do doctoral work.

At that point [1965], knowledge was coming out of the U.S., out of MIT, so I applied there. I told them that I had no money, and if they didn't give me a scholarship, I couldn't go. So they did. That was great, I was so fortunate that they gave me admission and offered me a teaching assistantship, I was very lucky to have that.

Life at MIT

I had fabulous professors; one of them was Prof. Bose, who started the Bose System. Amar Bose played a very large role in my life, he was highly regarded, his classes were legend. Before Bose, I had only heard of entrepreneurship, but here I saw a live person, to whom I was a teaching assistant.

I finished my Ph.D. in 1970 and I was invited to join the faculty both at Carnegie Mellon and MIT—both places were fantastic. I joined MIT and teaching was a very good possibility for me because I thought I could do that in India if I returned.

I was there for five years and did very, very interesting work and then I was attracted away to the University of Utah for microelectronics. I already knew three-quarters of the faculty professionally, and at the time, the university had a very strong department in Electronics; I stayed there for five years.

New Chip Design

There I undertook some research, which looked at newer ways of designing chips. There were two people in the country, Carver Meade out of Cal Tech and I, a computer architect from MIT. We had a method of using a higher level of design expressing what you want and translating it to chip design. This was a method of doing computer translation, which up to now had been done manually; it was called a silicon compiler and the area was design automation.

I had already developed methods and patents, and in Utah we were able to build these things to show that the theory actually worked. This attracted the attention of a large company that later funded us; it was called General Instrument Corporation. They had cable divisions and they needed to do whole systems on a chip.

At that time, General Instrument Corporation asked me to join them or do something with the new design methodology. I said, "Okay, but I will retain my university connection and start Patil Systems in Utah." It took me about three years in Utah to I realize that I needed to be here in Silicon Valley when it came to raising more funds.

Fabless Semiconductors

I came here to the Valley and got venture money in 1984. I was proposing to do something audacious which had not been done—and that was that we would be a semiconductor company without actually building a fab. Today it would be called a fabless semiconductor company. And for this, I was ridiculed by those guys who were so knowledgeable in the Silicon Valley, including the founder of AMD, who said, "Real men have fabs." [laughter]

People would say to us [Mike Hackworth became Patil's partner in 1985] "Oh, you can make nice samples, but you can never make production parts." There was no easy answer except to just do it! You have to make sure that in your enthusiasm, you are not walking off the cliff.

Success

Q: *How do you define success?*

A: To me success is not one thing, it has many dimensions. Success has been for me, on one side, professional success; it is to be able to follow a dream that otherwise would have been impossible; it is being able to achieve, this is life self-actuation, self-satisfaction.

The second one is to be able to make a difference, to have an impact. In fact, as a professor, if I made a difference where someone who had potential, actually could reach their potential with my help, I felt so good about it. That got transferred when I started a company to bring my ideas to fruition because no one else would do it, but I became extremely aware from the beginning that I was creating a livelihood for people—for that reason I simply had to succeed. That was the engine to give back to society.

Money is a part of life and it is necessary to make money, but when you have made that money, what can you do with it? The only thing you can do is to give it away. And give it away because that is the way you can influence and guide things that happen in society. So if you make money beyond your own needs, then you are in a position to contribute in a philanthropic way.

Chinese Tea

TIE (The Indus Entrepreneur)

Q: *Was this one of the reasons you founded TIE?*

A: Cirrus Logic was growing very rapidly and doing well; I was reaching middle age and becoming more reflective. We had reached a level of success that we had not dreamed would be possible. We had hopes and when our dreams came true, we said we wanted to do something.

I said, the Indo-American community is young, it has yet to define its values. That was one thing.

The second, we can give direct money, we can certainly give money (and we do), but really what we know much better is how to build a company. So if we could undertake giving back in such a way that those coming after us could learn from our school of hard knocks, it would be our—the Indo American community's—gift to the land which accepted us and of which we became a part. And, it would be open, it is not an Indian organization, we are proactively open.

The Beginnings of TIE

In the first years of TIE, I could fully utilize my learning as a founder, as an entrepreneur, as a teacher, as a professor and a consensus builder and I scratched my head and said, "How am I going to do this?" I thought we should have a common activity in which we could participate which when done, we could feel very good about.

So I proposed two things: in spring, let's have a conference—TIECON—to teach basic and advanced skills for beginners and for people who had taken the plunge. And, since we are in Silicon Valley and connected, we can get the best people to present. And everyone signed up.

The second one, I thought would be a financial conference in the fall, modeled after financial conferences where there are well known companies, financial institutions, break-out rooms and things like that.

We all worked together and we had a conference that was so well done, everything started on time and the design we had in mind actually came through. The community itself felt very proud because this was very professional and there was plenty of coverage in the weekly news.

Then we set out to do the hard work, the mentoring program, the monthly events and so on.

Advice for Entrepreneurs

Q: *What advice would you give to Indians living or coming here to the U.S to work who want to follow in your footsteps?*

A: Why just Indians?

Q: *Because you know what Indian culture might be better at.*

A: The Indians are in fairly good shape, I would say. It is actually more; I would like to give advice to the next generation of Indians or other cultures.

Morning Fog

Entrepreneurship

Entrepreneurship is actually a way of doing things, of professionally participating. My advice would be to educate yourself as much as you are able to. All the way to a Ph.D. and the rationale for that is entrepreneurial opportunities exist today, they will exist tomorrow and beyond your own lifetime.

These opportunities will be just different. It is a risky, intense endeavor, the rest of the world thinks about entrepreneurs as the wild risk takers, like Evil Knievel, who would run his motorcycle and jump over big buildings or canyons—one of those daredevils. Now, his act would go away, if you took his activity away.

The entrepreneur takes risks because he doesn't know how to go from here to there any other way; and after taking risks, he works, and if he found the path of lesser risk, he would take that path shamelessly. So if you want to mitigate risk, the best thing is to be prepared. The more you are prepared, the better; you never know at what stage risk comes to you, and once you have learned something, it never goes away.

In the phase of entrepreneurship, there is not much time for broad learning. What happens in a Ph.D., unlike in a Master's, you are confronted with doing it on your own. So the loneliness is like a solo flight, you have to confront your own ability, tenacity, motivation, where there are lots of unknowns; kind of sorting and finding your path and having the inner discipline—not be cocky, but yet be confident. All of these things you absolutely encounter when creating something new. What can be better training for being an entrepreneur than putting yourself through this otherwise very difficult experience of getting a Ph.D.?

Wu Fu Chen, Founding Partner of Genesis Campus and Acorn Campus

Wu-Fu Chen
Founding Partner of Genesis Campus and Acorn Campus
Country of Origin: Taiwan
Group: The Start-Up Wizards

> *"I think the start-up environment from many perspectives is easier than managing a large company. When people join start-ups, they aren't joining for higher salaries; rather, they are all in the same boat, so there are far less corporate politics."*

I was introduced to Wu Fu Chen with the help of my friend Shirley Lin, Chairwoman of the National Taiwan University Alumni Association, of which Mr. Chen and his wife Ellen are members.

Q: *Please tell us what you're doing professionally today?*

A: I'm moving more from being an entrepreneur to being an early-stage investor. I'm starting and investing in companies and also looking at the necessity of linking the U.S. and the rest of the world, particularly China and Taiwan, because I'm more familiar with them. I'm funding early-stage companies in the U.S., Taiwan and China.

Q: *Do you think at some point China can supplant Silicon Valley?*

A: I don't think China, by itself, will become another Silicon Valley. I think the U.S. and Silicon Valley still lead and have their strengths.

China with its fast growth will develop certain strengths, and in certain sectors, it may even surpass Silicon Valley—more likely it will be in areas such as the wireless space.

Family Beginnings

Q: *How did your family influence you?*

A: Back in my childhood, which was 40 or 50 years ago, Taiwan was pretty poor. I think coming from a poor family, you have this feeling that you want to get out of poverty and that certainly gave me the drive.

Q: *Was it more that you wanted to get out of where you were, or was it your parents saying that you had to study?*

A: Chinese families, we're like Jewish families. They always sacrifice for their children's education. China is moving so fast, partially because they're paying so much attention to education, because clearly the higher the education, the better to get out of poverty.

It's definitely true that the family was pushing me to get a good education and they asked me to study hard. They thought that was the only way to get out of poverty.

Education

Q: *What made you come to the U.S.?*

A: First, I was fortunate to go to the best university in Taiwan, Taiwan University, in the Electrical Engineering department. At that time, Taiwan didn't have very good higher education facilities, so the best thing was to go to the U.S. I had a pretty generous scholarship offer. Although I have to say, it's the best way for the United States to keep the best talents in the country.

Q: *How hard was it for you to leave this big family you have, to make the jump to the United States? And how was your English?*

A: My written English, back then, was pretty good, but orally, it was horrible, because there was no opportunity to practice it. Chinese always do well in the written part, as in the TOEFL. But when I got here, it was horrible. I remember the first airport I got to was LAX, and I realized I couldn't understand anything people were saying.

In fact, I remember my graduate school. I went to Florida for my Master's Degree and I actually took a tape recorder with me to record the classes to make sure that I did well. So with that, I got straight As and I worked very hard for that Master's Degree.

Q: *What did you do after that?*

After the Master's, I applied to the Ph.D. program in Berkeley. I wanted to continue my Ph.D., but I actually didn't finish. I didn't pass the preliminary exam. I was very frustrated and it was the first time, certainly, that I realized it was my English and it was not the hard questions in Computer Science they were asking that I had problems with. They asked me questions to express my opinion, rather than for me to talk about mathematics. I didn't do well because of my English and I didn't pass.

Focus on Career

Q: *What did you do then?*

A: I decided to find a job. It was pretty easy to find a job in San Francisco, in the downtown area. It was my first interview; I went to the placement center and they made a call. I was hired to do sales support for teller-terminals for banks. At the time, in 1976, I was 26.

While I was in the company, I was the only one doing the technical support. The rest of the people were in sales. So I was following the Money String Theory—the closer to the money, the easier to get it. As an engineer, you're in the back office, not close to the money. So I decided that I had to do one of two things: move up in the corporate ladder or start my own company, so I could get more into the decision making process.

That's when I decided I wanted to go do a start-up. I knew I didn't have the experience then, nor did I have the money to start my own company back then, so I decided I first had to build up my experience. I decided to invest ten years of my time to get ready for a start-up.

The 10-Year Plan

Q: *So you had a real plan in your head?*

A: Yes, definitely. My only strength was my technical background and I was an EE and Computer Science major. I knew the computer world well enough, but I didn't have the experience building a computer. I decided to call a company called Harris Corporation in Fort Lauderdale, Florida.

I was pretty lucky, whenever I interviewed for a job, I was always accepted; and I decided to pick the company not based on the salary. I knew what I wanted and it wasn't dependent on the salary. I wanted to be able to build an operating system from the ground up because I think that's the most important part of the computer, it's the brain of the computer.

In the second year, I decided that once you know the brain of the computer, you still have that information structure or the databases to learn. So I decided to find a job in the area of database management. A guy at Wang Laboratories wanted to do that. They started it and I was hired into that group in Boston.

Q: *Did you have connections to get into that group? Did you know the right people?*

A: Once I decided that I was looking for database management, I looked in the newspaper. I found the company; I went to the interview and was accepted. So I spent two years learning how to build databases, to understand how the data are arranged and built by the computer.

The next thing I wanted to learn was about communication. I think the timing was perfect for me. When I decided to do that, Wang Labs started a communications division, which was pretty early. They had Wang Net—this was in 1981. I stayed there for two years.

Working on an MBA

While I was working at Wang, I was taking MBA classes in finance at night. I had decided it was not necessary to take classes for a degree; what I needed to get was the knowledge of finance related business management.

After that, I had decided to join a start-up to learn how to start a company because I thought I had the basics and the technical background. I was lucky to find a start-up company with only four people and they hired me. I was the first software engineer hired.

One of the founders of Bytex came from the same National Taiwan University; based on our common background, he had some confidence in me and he was willing to hire me even though he thought I didn't have enough experience. The company later went public but I left after five years, before the IPO. The reason I left was I knew I was about ready to do my own start-up.

At that point, my 10-year plan to create my own start-up had been shortened to eight years. I was ahead of my schedule by two years. I had stayed in this company for five years and in the other two companies for three years, and now I was ready to start my own company.

First Start-Up

Q: *Had you had the idea of what you wanted to do or did you get the idea of the new company while you were working?*

A: The idea came while I was working. You can't have an idea for a very long time before someone else comes up with the same idea. The product concept really came only a year before I left Bytex. But doing my first company was still pretty hard, a lot of hard work.

And it did not come out as well as I had expected it to. Looking back, it was too technically driven. I was a technical person and when I left Bytex Corporation, I was the head of R&D; a few technical people came with me to start the new company. Based on our experience at

Bytex, we knew how to build a better product, but building a better product didn't turn out to be enough.

We ended up building a good technology, but a good technology and a good product aren't enough because the market is not just looking at the product, but also at all the pieces and the company.

New Directions

A year later, I went back to Taiwan. I had not been back in 15 years. During the two weeks I was in Taiwan, I read, by accident, an article in the newspaper about a company of one of my classmates and so I called him—he was head of the company D-Link. It is a very famous networking company. And after we chatted a while, he said, "Why don't we start a company together?" So I went back to the United States and wrote a business plan. That one, called Cameo, was located in Taiwan, so I had to commute from Boston to Taiwan for about a year.

After a year's commute, I decided to ask my younger brother to run the company and I started another company in Boston. So far, that was the most successful one; it actually went public less than four years after its inception.

Meanwhile, Ed Anderson was calling me. Knowing my company was sold and I had decided to leave, he teamed me up with another person, Desh Deshpande. We started Cascade Communications; he was responsible for marketing and I was responsible for engineering and R&D.

After we built the product, we brought in another CEO and it went public in three and a half years. The market cap went over $10 billion. After it went public, I decided to move on. I was managing 500 engineers and that was not my interest, so I left and started another company called Arris Networks, which provided Internet access to people, allowing them to dial in via modem; this was on a large scale, for people to dial in and access the network.

Arris Networks was acquired within six months for over $150 million by Cascade Communications. In fact, Cisco wanted to acquire it for more money, but we decided to go with Cascade. They saw that this was such a good idea, that they decided that they didn't have to wait for us to develop the product. Our track record showed that we would be able to build the product.

Success

Q: *What does it mean to you to be successful?*

A: First, I wanted to be financially independent, which happened pretty soon. Bytex, even though I left, went public, and I still owned some stock and Cascade was also a huge success, so I don't have to do anything anymore. I really enjoy entrepreneurship and starting something from nothing, so I always continue looking for and initiating something new. After building it to a certain stage, I don't mind handing it over to other people.

Global Leadership

Q: *What is the most important thing to know about multicultural or global leadership?*

A: The world is getting smaller and smaller now. For Chinese and most Asians coming here, we tend to work pretty hard. They're mostly technical people, they're quiet and they don't express their opinion much. They typically don't move around. It's hard to see them moving up and becoming managers. The glass ceiling is pretty low. In Eastern culture, you're educated not to be vocal, not to express yourself.

Advice

Q: *What advice would you give to Chinese here? How can Chinese men and woman move up through the glass ceiling?*

A: I went through that difficulty, one was cultural and one was language. The Chinese language is so different from English, so it's hard to excel in English. And because of that, you tend to be held back. That happened to me, I failed in Berkeley and I was disappointed because I always had done very well academically before. I couldn't believe that I hadn't passed to get into the Ph.D. program. That really taught a lesson that I really needed to improve my English. That's when I decided to step out of the university and take the opportunity to improve myself.

The advice I'd give to Chinese is that they should learn English so that they can express themselves well and learn to network. Both of my kids are doing an MBA and both of them are working for start-ups. The MBA is important for networking.

My son applied to four schools: Berkeley, Stanford, Harvard and the Chinese-European International Business School in Shanghai, it's ranked number one in Asia right now and 11th in the world. If you do Stanford and Harvard, you're really connected to the best people. In the next 10 or 20 years, Asia will be important, so it's good to start connecting with both sides, i.e., Asia and the U.S. Right now, for Chinese and any other cultural group, the opportunity is much better because people tend to be able to accept other ethnicities.

Find your own path. Ideally, it is different from the one others take so that you can be ahead.

Dina Bitton, VP, SAP

Dina Bitton
VP, SAP
Country of Origin: France
Group: The Start-Up Wizards

> *"It is much harder for a woman to raise capital than for a man. If you look at the number of companies that are run by women and you look at the portion of venture capital that goes to women you will see a great discrepancy—less than four percent of all venture capital goes to women-led companies."*

Dina Bitton and I know each other from L'Executive Club events. Dina is such a quiet, self-effacing woman, it is amazing to see she hasn't had just one successful start-up, but three!

Q: *How would you describe what you are doing today?*

A: I am the Vice President in the technology division of SAP specializing in integration of information. We have a new division called EIM for Enterprise Information Management.

Selling Her Company

Q: *How did selling your company to SAP work out?*

A: We connected Callixa to different SAP products. We wanted to provide unified access to information from SAP systems as well as non-SAP systems.

Childhood Experiences

Q: *How did your childhood experiences or your family influence your choice of career?*

A: Actually it was a very unexpected turn of events. I grew up in French Morocco, went to a French school and was headed to study French literature. But then, my family immigrated to Israel after Morocco got its independence from the French. I also liked mathematics and physics and it made a lot more sense to pursue a scientific degree rather than a literary one. So I went to college at the Technion Institute in Israel. I studied there for five years and I got two degrees: an undergraduate degree and a Master's Degree in Mathematics.

Obstacles

Q: *Where were some of the obstacles you had to overcome in your continuing career? And how did you get from Israel to California?*

A: The languages were the most challenging. First I had to go from French Morocco and France to Israel. I didn't speak Hebrew and had to learn the language. I actually came to the U.S. to go to graduate school in Computer Science. At that time I went to the University of Wisconsin, in Madison. It was a very cold climate coming out of Morocco and Israel and then going to the U.S.—it was kind of a shock.

First Woman on Engineering Faculty

I got a Ph.D. in Computer Science in 1981; then I was offered a post-doctoral fellowship in Israel at the Weizman Institute where I spent a year. Later I was offered a faculty position at Cornell University; I think I became the first woman in the College of Engineering, on the faculty of the College of Engineering. There were about 600 male faculty members. I stayed there for three years, then I was offered tenure at the University of Illinois and I moved to Chicago as a tenured professor in Computer Science.

Move to Silicon Valley

Three years later, I took a sabbatical year and came to Stanford University. Then the obvious choice was to do a start-up because that's what everyone did around here [laughter].

Q: *How did you go about it?*

A: I had attended a conference where I exhibited a prototype of a system I had built with my graduate students and there was significant interest in the prototype. It moved very fast. I was about to secure venture capital and hired several of my graduate students. That was my first trial doing a start-up in Silicon Valley. We developed a product and very soon the company, DB Software, was acquired by a larger company, which was East Coast-based Cadre Technology. They wanted to diversify their product portfolio by acquiring this DB Software. I worked for the acquiring company for about a year on the West Coast, in the same place. They kept the whole team here. After a year, I decided to do another start-up.

Second Start-Up

In 1998, I started a second company which was subsequently renamed Evoke Software. I had a different idea. I ran that company for about four years. At Evoke, I was the founder and CEO for three years and then you know it was time to extend the company, and the investors wanted to bring in a new CEO with a background in sales and marketing. We did that and I stayed on as the CTO for a year and then I decided to move on and start another venture.

Third Start-Up

So this was start-up number three. You know by then I had learned the works. I built a great team and raised a large amount of venture capital even though the bubble had already burst, I closed 15 million dollars in a Series A round.

Q: *So the VCs knew you and had confidence in what you did?*

A: It is much harder for a woman to raise capital than for a man. People like to invest with people who are like them, or network with them and are in the mainstream. If you look at the number of companies that are run by women and you look at the portion of venture capital that goes to women you will see a great discrepancy—less than four percent of all venture capital goes to women-led companies.

Success as a Woman

Q: *What does it mean to be successful?*

A: Different people feel differently about it, especially in Silicon Valley. Very often success is equal to how much wealth you have accumulated. That has never been my primary goal, even though I have been able to accumulate some wealth. My passion has always been creating something different as well as creating a good work environment and having a good rapport with people.

Q: *When did you feel "I made it"? When was that moment?*

A: Basically never. There is always the next thing you want to do, otherwise you just wither and die.

Role of Silicon Valley

Q: *Could you have become successful outside of the Silicon Valley?*

A: Being an entrepreneur outside Silicon Valley is much more difficult, access to capital is much more limited. I could probably have done something similar in Israel. Israel is also a hotbed of technology, even though it was not yet at the time I left.

Advice to Young Professionals

Q: *If you were to give advice to others coming to Silicon Valley?*

A: You really have to open your mind and be very alert to picking up on the way business is conducted here. It is very human to think, "In my country, we do it better." Even if we don't admit it, we tend to react that way. There is a reason why people come here. They should never forget that it is a privilege to be here, to have access to so many opportunities.

Q: *What would you tell women, in particular young women?*

A: It is much harder for women. There is no denying that. That is why a few years ago I helped found an organization called "The Women's Technology Cluster" (WTC, now known as ASTIA). The purpose of the WTC is to help women entrepreneurs in high tech and biotech, by providing them mentoring, coaching, access to financial networks, review of business plans.

Samba Murthy, Founder and COO, Xambala

Samba Murthy
Founder and COO, Xambala[10]
Country of Origin: India
Group: The Start-Up Wizards

> *"You have to get out of your comfort zone. Because life is not just spice and curry, you know. There are other things, so keep an open mind."*

When I joked with Samba, that Henry Wong designed companies on napkins in restaurants, he told me he actually did his on a white paper around his kitchen table and in a proverbial garage as well!

Q: *What do you do at your company, Xambala [pronounced Shamba-la]?*

A: Xambala is a Tibetan word that means "Shangri-La." Xambala is a technology company and we are building a fundamental processing engine that will allow you to convert digital bits into information.

---

10. Samba has since moved to a non-operations role at Xambala as Board member and is now working on two new start-up ventures. He is also actively engaged with three start-ups as an adviser.

Previous Ventures

Q: *Have you run a company before?*

A: Yes, I did that at XaQti [pronounced Shakti] as well, I was the founding CEO. And I recruited Henry Wong to come and take over and run it. What I like to do is create new things, solve new problems, and have fun doing it. I am now responsible for engineering operations, basically for all the technology, product development.

Childhood Influences

Q: *How did your childhood experiences in your family influence where you are today?*

A: I consider myself very fortunate in that both my dad, mom and my grandparents (both sets) were all very well-educated. They were brought up in a very middle class environment. They brought themselves up the hard way. They knew education was important, and my dad's side of the family, my grandfather was a lawyer.

Q: *So you were very studious?*

A: No, the interesting thing is, I was allowed to mess up. I ran wild—literally. I did great in high school, but in engineering school I was partying and having a lot of fun. My dad's approach was very simple, "Look, you can have fun, but I don't want to hear any excuses about you flunking out. As long as your grades are all right you can do whatever you want."

Q: *But you were young.*

A: Yes, I was quite young. Let's see, I think it was '78. I was 21 when I graduated from engineering school with the engineering degree. So I bounced around and it also allowed me to find out what I enjoy. The bottom line is though, the family tolerated my escapades. That was important.

Education and First Jobs

Q: *What did you do after graduation?*

A: I worked in a company called BHEL, which is kind of like General Electric here in the U.S. It's a very large, public company in India and what they do is considered a big deal.

Q: *Do many people from IITs get in there?*

A: Yes and from other institutions as well. I graduated from one of the two oldest engineering schools in India, ASIA, which was started during the old British days. It's a 220-year-old school at this point, my grandfather graduated from there, my father graduated from there. I am the third generation from that school.

Road to the U.S.

Q: *How did you get to the United States?*

A: In '82, my younger brother graduated and he came to the U.S. He asked, "What are you doing? You should show up in the U.S." In fact, I didn't want to bother applying but he pushed me to apply to a few schools anyway.

I ended up in the South Dakota School of Mines and Technology in Rapid City, South Dakota.

There were a couple of high profile Indian professors there in Civil Engineering and Computer Science and I knew some folks who had graduated from there previously. The first semester I was on my own, in the second semester I managed to get some ways to fund myself and I got a teaching assistantship, teaching microcomputer lab.

Q: *So you were going for a Master's Degree?*

A: Yes, in Electrical Engineering.

Q: *What happened then?*

A: At the end of '85, I headed to San Jose, California looking for a job, and stayed with an alumnus friend who was kind and generous enough to host me and my wife.

I ended up with a job at SEEQ technology. SEEQ was the first company which had built Ethernet chips for Ethernet networking. They built the first chips for a company called 3Com founded by Bob Metcalfe and much later led by Eric Benhamou.

Q: *You were at the right place at the right time.*

A: I got lucky. SEEQ, was founded by a few ex-Intel engineers. They invented the first commercial implementation techniques for electrically erasable programmable floating gate memories. They left Intel and started SEEQ to commercialize EEPROMs.

Timing is Everything

Q: *You seem to have been in all the right places.*

A: Timing is everything and I guess I was fortunate there. SEEQ as a company had a very checkered financial history, ups and downs. They had a great IPO and then they went through several industry inflection points: entry of the Japanese memory suppliers, manufacturing industry migration, move to a fabless chip model.

First Start-Up

Q: *And when did you leave to get to your first start-up?*

A: In '95. The seeds got planted in the '93 time frame because I ran into a company called Kalpana which Cisco bought later to get into the Ethernet switching business.

Kalpana went through the typical bumpy ride as a start-up company. Before they got bought by Cisco, a whole bunch of people left to do another start-up. We wanted to do better scalable solutions, so Alak [Deb] started telling me "Let's do something." But I wasn't sure.

Q: *What did you do?*

A: In mid '95, I got tired of the status quo at SEEQ. There was another start-up company which decided that they wanted me. So I decided to leave SEEQ and the right time came up with Alak. I told Alak, "Look, let's talk. Let's start with a blank sheet, let's do something creative."

Q: *Not a napkin? Henry Wong does that on napkins. [laughter]*

A: No, we actually did it on a white paper or a blank sheet, or whatever you want to call it. We did do this around our kitchen dinner table and Alak's proverbial garage as well. We tried to get corporate funding first. It was a painful year and a half.

Q: *So how did you get funded?*

A: Andy Bechtolsheim [Sun Co-Founder, see his interview], Alak and I, and a few other well known industry folks like Bobby Johnson (Foundry Networks CEO) and Gordon Stitt (Extreme Networks CEO), got together off of highway 237, at a hotel place now called the Crown Plaza and we had a meeting. The meeting was actually arranged by some ex-Packet Engines folks in the late summer of '96.

Henry Wong showed up at this meeting too. He was sitting in the back. Nobody knew what we were up to; we were all doing these skunk works. I had actually sold some stuff to Henry some time in the past during my SEEQ days. In the meantime, Alak and I were trying hard to raise money. Henry pitched to me with very simple logic. "I have no technology, but I can raise money. You folks have the technology." So we said, "You're sure you can raise money?" We all sat down, and after a lot of discussion over many cups of coffee at the Red Lion Hotel in San Jose, we agreed to work together.

Q: *And what was the name of the company?*

We named the company "XaQti" which stands for "Switching (X) acceleration with Queuing Transport Interfaces." "XaQti" means "power" in multiple Indian languages; in Tamil, in Hindi, Bengali.

Success is Being Self-Sufficient

Q: *What does it then mean to you to have been successful?*

A: Success is a couple of things: one is being self-sufficient. I no longer have constraints, only my own self-inflicted wounds, if you will, on that.

It has never been so much about the money. The goal for me on a personal level is to make sure that on my family side, my wife and children and I have a financial structure which is safe enough—that's one part of it. The other part is to be able to point to my business, and say, "I did that—I accomplished that." Something that had an impact on a personal level, something that I had contributed. It didn't matter to me whether people acknowledged it or not, as long as I felt I had done something good that I was happy about—that was success for me.

Silicon Valley's Role

Q: *Could you have been as successful outside of Silicon Valley?*

A: You know, it's a hypothetical question. In Silicon Valley, the probability of success is a lot higher than anywhere else. The ecosystem here fosters alliances for start-up success. For example, my other Co-Founder at Xambala, Rajan Raghavan, provided the back end services for XaQti.

The system here is pretty straightforward. You have an open shot at it. There are no stumbling blocks so you can maneuver around it. You can worry about focusing on the task at hand instead of worrying about a lot of extraneous things. You know what works, what does not.

I think places like China and India are also coming along, but I think they are probably 20 years behind. We have a design center in India, and I used to work in India. Coming after 15+ years, there is a monumental world of change. You look at it; there are still a lot of obstacles, impediments to success, if you will. There is still a lot of red tape. Silicon Valley does give you that edge, I think.

Leadership

Q: *What are the most important things to keep in mind when you are a leader?*

A: Okay, Rule number one: integrity and honest communications. Very important to get everyone on the same page. That means communication is important, and you better line up everybody so they are running/rowing in the same direction. It is very, very important and critical to success to make sure the objectives are understood by everybody.

The objectives need to line up and be tied together in some intangible ways to personal goals and objectives of individuals. If employees are not convinced that they are headed in the right direction, they are going to spin in circles. It takes an effort to convey the objectives and get everyone in sync.

The second rule is: right people at the right job. Make sure you have the right people doing the right task. I find that hard. The reason is very simply that people are humans; to a large extent, when you put people into tasks, you find there are mismatches.

The third one is persistence. You can have a plan, but it's your ability, as they say, to tackle and block and to maneuver. I like to use the sailing analogy: you have to go with the wind direction, you keep making progress and you have to tack. And you have to be persistent; persistence alone wins.

Advice to Indian Immigrants

Q: *What advice would you give to Indians coming to the Valley or living here?*

A: The biggest problem with Indians is they tend to focus just on Indians and it takes an enormous kind of effort to get over this cultural handicap. The tendency is to flock together. You have to get out of your comfort zone. Because life is not just spice and curry, you know. There are other things, so keep an open mind.

Chapter

6 The Corporate Wizards

The risk-taking Start-Up Wizards might be the poster children for Silicon Valley. But there are equally accomplished immigrants working inside corporations. Their career choices might appear less risky. But they have often taken a unique approach to their career to establish themselves as leaders inside their companies.

They are accomplished players on the world stage who use their positions of influence inside global companies to drive growth in innovative and exciting ways.

Their sensitivity to different cultures often makes them incredibly effective managers within their own companies, around Silicon Valley, and across the globe.

These people tell the story of the Corporate Wizards:

- Alex Vieux, Publisher and CEO, Red Herring
- Allen Wang, CMO, Google Asia
- Aliza Peleg, Managing Director, SAP Labs
- Chi Foon Chan, President and COO, Synopsys

- Omid Kordestani, SVP Global Sales and Business Development, Google
- Marc Onetto, SVP, Solectron
- Miriam Rivera, Lawyer, Google
- Qi Lu, SVP, Yahoo!
- Shantanu Narayen, President and COO, Adobe Systems
- Sarit Firon, CFO, Olive Software

Alex Vieux, Publisher and CEO, Red Herring

Alex Vieux
Publisher and CEO, Red Herring
Country of Origin: France
Group: The Corporate Wizards

> *"Despite this diversity, or maybe because of it, the collective dream of Silicon Valley remains the same 25 years later."*

Waiting to speak to Alex (who had just arrived from another trip) was well worth it, as he is one of the unique figures in the Silicon Valley. I have attended panels he moderated. He is someone who really knows his craft.

Red Herring

Q: *What does being the publisher and CEO of Red Herring involve?*

A: Publishing *Red Herring* and being the CEO of *Red Herring* are two different functions, right? One of them takes care of the magazine, it tries to identify ways to reach more readers with more and better content, and to find a way to talk to the best people and have access to them so that our journalists manage to get the best stories to write.

And on the other hand, I have to look at how to be economically profitable for everyone and to make money, sell advertising, get projects or special issues, which will create a new wave of content for people.

Q: *How long have you been in the United States?*

A: 21 years now.

Family Background

Q: *What role did your family play in your career?*

A: My father was a diplomat, my mother went to the university, was a professor. My father was writing books, my mother was writing books. They were writers, they were intellectuals; they valued the idea of writing, researching and sharing their intellect with the world. I had parents who, by definition, because of their jobs, were very social, especially my mother. She knew everyone around and everyone knew her.

Q: *Where did you grow up?*

A: In Paris, in Zaire, in Mali...My father was a United Nations diplomat, so we went to places very few knew where to find on the map. It was a very interesting time.

Education

Q: *What kind of education did you have?*

A: I was educated in France. I went to one of those posh boarding schools when I was thirteen. We rode horses and this and that...the lake, the forest...it was a beautiful and amazing time. Then I went to HEC and Sciences Po, two illustrious French institutions. I got a Master's Degree there and in five years I was done. I moved very quickly and at 24, I was done with all of this.

Coming to the U.S.

I went to work with Andersen Consulting for three years, while also teaching at the Sorbonne. At 27, I decided to come to the United States.

Q: *Did you come to California immediately?*

A: Yes, I went to Stanford Business School from 1985 to 1987 and I was working for *Le Monde* and *L'Expansion*. Before 1985, I used to come to the United States three or four times a year because I worked for Andersen Consulting. I wanted to work in American firms, because I thought I would get better training.

New Directions

Q: *What did you do after you got your MBA?*

A: It was a very interesting time. I had offers from the Boston Consulting Group and Bain Consulting. Instead, I wanted to become an entrepreneur, so I joined a friend of mine and together we started a company. And the company eventually went public and I started a second company, which eventually got sold.

One of them involved financial software and since I was not a trader, I learned finance. I knew software somehow because at Andersen Consulting I was used to using a computer. I was on the consulting side for three years. I was not an engineer but I knew enough to process the thing.

ETRE

Q: *That was the first business you did; what was the second?*

A: The same thing: a software company. I created two software companies—CATZ and Renaissance Software. And then after four years, I started ETRE—the European Technology Roundtable Exhibition—the biggest conference in the world. ETRE became the "Davos" for the industry. In French, être means "to be." This was an existential message. We still run it every year. Every year it changes its location within Europe.

Challenges on the Way to Success

Q: *What does it mean to you to be successful?*

A: I believe in humility. I'm not saving lives, I'm not putting three million dollars toward creating a vaccine, I'm not helping kids in Mongolia, or kids in Haiti or in Senegal, who don't have a chance to survive their first year; so I just want to be sure that people know that my definition of success is in a small pond. I'm not a Leonardo Da Vinci. There is an intellectual problem of finding one or two key ideas which people are going to refer to for the next five centuries.

A Private Connecting Machine

Q: *What are you proud of?*

A: Of ETRE and of what we have done on a daily basis. You would not believe it but every day I get people stopping me in the street or at dinner and they say, "You know, because of you, I went to see that person, and that person gave me this and that thing led to that."

We are a private and a public service. We are a private connecting machine. We are connectors. We are connectors of the new way because we don't just create events, we facilitate them.

Silicon Valley

Q: *Would you have been successful in disseminating your ideas and passions if you had been anywhere else but the Silicon Valley?*

A: Sometimes I want to say yes. Because you carry what you are anywhere you go. I was ready even in France. Wherever I would have carried out my ideas, things might have been different. Maybe I would have done something else or embraced another career. Maybe I would have dedicated my energy to public service. Maybe I would have become a politician. If you could measure economically how much you help, I think that I might have helped many people in an alternative role as much as I am doing now.

America gave me a chance not only to do a lot of things professionally, but to dream out loud and to make those things come true. If you had told me ten years ago that today I would be the CEO and Publisher of *Red Herring*, an iconic publication which epitomizes the technology industry, I would not have believed you. Who am I? I'm the fourth gun of this industry; I've met more people than I deserve—so every day I say to myself, especially when I am sad and when things are not going my way and I have difficult moments or family problems, whatever they are—when those things happen, I say to myself, "Come on, come on. What a journey."

Foreign Influences

Q: *How did you think Silicon Valley changed as a result of foreign influences?*

A: Silicon Valley, in the past 25 years, has gone from very clubbish to being very international. At the time I first encountered the Sand Hill Road entrepreneurs, I observed that a large percentage of them were white men.

Today it's a different world out there. There still aren't enough women, but you have Chinese, you have Indians, we still don't have Blacks, but there are some Hispanics. The world has changed, we have progressed. I can tell you this is an amazing thing. Fifty percent of the companies go public after they've been started or are run by a CEO born outside of this country.

Silicon Valley has changed radically. One, it has absorbed a lot of people at the leadership level and has given them the chance to be trained, to be meshed, and to accomplish things. That is something that no other country has done.

Q: *What do you mean by, "they have been meshed?"*

A: I mean they are part of the mélange. They are totally integrated. Go to school in Menlo Park or Los Altos Hills and you will become aware of the kids of Mr. Johnson and the kids of Mr. Schneider—they all go to the same school, so they are meshed. And their kids are going out with each other now. They are sixteen, seventeen and eighteen. They don't even think about it. They are going to have children with each other. What a beautiful world.

This is the thing that you have when you go to Israel. You have Israelis from the West, Israelis from the East, Israelis from the South, Israelis from the Arab world, Israelis coming from Poland. And all of them from the same school. And I tell myself, this is the next Brazil. This is beautiful, and I think this is a great thing.

Silicon Valley Dreams

The second thing which is interesting is that Americans in Silicon Valley continue to open themselves and keep the dream alive. Silicon Valley has changed in that now in every company, you have people from fifteen nations, and everyone is a contributor. Despite this diversity, or maybe because of it, the collective dream of Silicon Valley remains the same 25 years later.

What amazes me is even with the large number of people, the dream remains the same for everyone. They can make it. There's a next new thing and they will be part of it. Silicon Valley has been incredible at not changing its potential. Foreigners here are embracing it and have made it even clearer that everybody can do it. Everybody can do it because a guy who comes from Iran and barely speaks English can build a large company and a guy from Russia can create Google. "Why not me? Why can't I?" people think. And it's the "why not me" which is great. Silicon Valley means: "why not me."

Advice to French Entrepreneurs

Q: *Which comes to the question, what do you think the French coming here need to do to be happy?*

A: Just go for it. Just forget everything else and go for it, and just run. Just run. You remember Forrest Gump? Forest Gump ran to the end of the country and came back. Until he wanted to stop; he stopped.

If you want to get an education, I would advise people to get an education here, because you get exposed to different ways of learning. Learn how the Americans learn. Use what you have learned elsewhere but do things as they do them here. People are very pragmatic; they have to be because they come from so many different backgrounds. Just use the pragmatisms and use your intelligence to move to the next step. Be patient.

Difference to Americans

Q: *What do you think foreign professionals have done differently or would do differently than Americans here in the Valley would have?*

Many of the foreigners here came from a culture of failure, a culture where it is more important to fear failure than to enjoy success. And by the way, if you earn success in Europe, people are very fearful of the way you did it. The culture, the dominating gene in Europe, is failure.

People who come from overseas have an edge because they have to face a lot of people who are skeptical all the time. Just because they left their place shows how utterly developed their power of conviction is. They have to take a risk.

Q: *Do you think that Silicon Valley will continue to attract foreigners? Or do you think that now, in China, for example, there are more possibilities?*

A: If I were 20 today, I would still come here. But I know that I would spend a few years in Hong Kong or Bangalore. The world does not care that I don't go to Europe. But it's not just one continent versus the other. Tomorrow you'll have more Americans going to Europe because that is where they can carve out better time and space for their personal lives or whatever. In the end, I think that people will continue coming to Silicon Valley because it is still a romantic place for many entrepreneurs.

Allen Wang, CMO, Google Asia

Allen Wang
CMO, Google Asia[11]
Country of Origin: China
Group: The Corporate Wizards

> *"Absorb as much culture as you can wherever you go, whether it's the U.S. or a European country, absorb the cultures, learn the academics and learn everything up to whatever role you want to play."*

I talked to Allen Wang via the phone from Beijing. A young Chinese entrepreneur had put me in touch with Allen, who is on the board of his start-up. This is networking in action, Silicon Valley style.

---

11. Allen Wang left Google in 2006 and has since founded his own company.

Q: *What is your current position?*

A: I am currently the Chief Marketing Officer for Google, Asia. In this job, I cover the whole Asian market. It is just great to have a Chinese playing the role of APAC chief marketing officer covering not just the Chinese market, but also Asian markets such as Japan and Korea.

Q: *How did your English come to be so excellent? You must have studied here.*

A: Well, my major in college was English. All in all, I've spent about 15 years in the U.S., the initial 22 years in China and then 15 plus years in the West. So I am pretty balanced in terms of my cultural range.

Q: *How did your childhood experiences and your family influence where you are today?*

A: I think I benefited from having a mother who was quite educated and always wanted her children to excel in whatever they did and, her work attitude was actually perfection, which helped. Then I watched my father who was a civil engineer by training, he rose to the head of the company and, in the end, he led about 2000 people. I was able to observe and appreciate him managing a large group of people, making an impact that way.

Q: *What was your educational path?*

A: I grew up in Beijing. I went to local Chinese schools, all really good ones. Today the schools are still very competitive from elementary to high school. After college at Tsinghua University in Beijing, I went to three places in the U.S. Columbia University in New York City was my first stop. After a year at Columbia I went to Carnegie Mellon, studying Computer-Mediated Cross-Cultural Negotiation. It was a communication thing. The final stop was Georgetown University where I attended their Business School. That was my formal training. I worked in the middle of it as a reporter for the Voice of America.

Career Moves

Q: *Why the Voice of America?*

A: I grew up listening to the Voice of America, in both Chinese and English. When I joined VOA, I just thought it was a good way to help the Chinese get information that they would otherwise not have had the privilege of getting. I worked there as a Chinese language reporter for two plus years, before going back to school at Georgetown.

And then in 1995, I interned at McKinsey and I spent a summer in their New York and Hong Kong offices.

After McKinsey, I joined another consulting company, Monitor Consulting. It was founded by a couple of Harvard business school professors; the leading founder was Michael Porter who authored a lot of groundbreaking strategy works. I did that for one year but I wasn't really happy with the theoretical kind of angle. I joined Proctor and Gamble in the U,S, headquarters in Cincinnati, Ohio, as brand manager getting a really classical dose of market training.

Q: *You were probably still pretty young at that point.*

A: No, at that point I was 33 years old. I left P&G after our first son was born. Cincinnati was becoming a place where—from a diversity point of view—not much was happening.

I moved to Silicon Valley where I joined Intuit. I only worked at Intuit for one year before I joined Yahoo!. I was at Yahoo! for almost four years, rising to the head of marketing for the Search and Marketplace Business Unit, the biggest business within Yahoo!, competing directly with Google, Amazon, eBay and other leading U.S. Web companies.

Moving to China

I came back to China in May 2006 to head up two things: one role I had was general manager at the head of their auction business; and in another role, I was head of North Asia Marketing.

Q: *So how did you get to Google?*

A: I joined Google because Yahoo! had decided to sell their operations to a local Chinese company called Alibaba.

Their philosophy was based on the painful realization—probably the right realization—that a multinational company that is headquartered outside China will have a tremendous amount of hardship, over time, managing a company in China.

No matter what amount of empowerment can happen, multinationals will not adequately understand the market. But Yahoo!'s solution was drastic. They said, "We are no longer managing anymore, we are the investor, we want to find a Chinese partner who can manage it for us." That is just what they did.

I still wanted to stay in China. The best place where I could immediately leverage what I had learned and where I could contribute was at Google. Google at this point was just entering China.

Q: *What were the biggest obstacles you had to overcome to get to where you are today?*

A: I would say two or three things quickly come to mind. One is I think to really do a good job with marketing discipline or as a general manager, I had to overcome the narrow scope of education, the narrow orientation I had been given when I first came out of China. The Chinese education system, it was more true then than it is now, trains very good technicians, but they don't really train thinkers. Of course, in their college years and very early on, students are trained to become experts in technical ways for a niche discipline.

I don't think that when we Chinese grow up we are encouraged in particular to speak our mind or to think out of the box. That is a big barrier. I have become quite conscious myself trying to overcome this.

If you look at the stuff I did, I zigged and zagged quite a lot. I think in doing all of this, I was somewhat consciously choosing that path not knowing where I would end up, but sort of knowing that crossing disciplines in that way would get me prepared for something.

I knew that this "something" was roughly in the managerial area. My professional growth happened in the U.S. At the beginning, I was a very good technician. I followed orders and I was not a good thinker. In order to become an outstanding kind of stand-up leader, you have to overcome this kind of inertia and shyness in terms of not being willing to speak up unless you have a better idea than anyone else.

Public Speaking

I definitely became aware of having to overcome shyness and I watched a lot of TV speeches by Ronald Reagan over and over again. I didn't necessarily agree with his philosophy but I definitely learned from him as a public speaker. I also watched tons of speeches by John Kennedy.

And, I paid a lot of attention to U.S. presidents who were eloquent orators, as for instance, Lincoln in his Gettysburg address. I picked up a lot, not just how to do public speaking, but how to actually have the right composure, how to cut in, how to join and drive an otherwise loosely composed team to some sort of a common goal—get them all fired up.

Q: *So you learned to share a vision?*

A: Yes, you were talking originally about difficult challenges. So having a vision with fire in the belly coupled with clear vision, a great charismatic vision with an overall great style. That was a challenge, that's number two.

Number three was the hard part, it was getting used to the Internet. The Internet works in a very different way; it is faster and it actually relies on less data, less thinking and more intuition. When I moved into the Internet world, in the first five or six months, I was really struggling. I had to temporarily throw everything out of the window in order to adjust. But once I adjusted, I found that what I had learned in the past certainly was applicable.

Success

Q: *How do you define success? What does success mean to you?*

A: Success is a multi-dimensional thing. It is foremost about making an impact. Making an impact in catapulting your company to the leading industry position, positively impacting the lives of others around you, including your family and coworkers.

I would also define success as a level of satisfaction that comes from seeing your end users happily using your services and products.

Third, having some sort of inner peace—you are giving your best because you are sure of your mission, not because of any outside pressure, or feeling insecure; not out of the necessity of making a living, but out of sheer enjoyment of the first two things: making an impact and satisfying the users. It comes out of the feeling that you are still able to balance what is work and what is life. Working is a hard thing to balance.

Multicultural Leadership Traits

Q: *What do you see the as the greatest challenge in multicultural leadership today?*

A: I think the courage to realize, no matter how much you know, how much you try to learn, you can never be able to become like the native in the culture that you are working in.

Advice for your Future

Q: *What advice would you give to Chinese—either Chinese who are going back to China to work, or Chinese who come to work in Silicon Valley?*

A: Say for example, they are very young and they come to the U.S. for college. I would say, "When you come here, you won't be able to see your future clearly. The future is really far away. Nobody but you can really find the future for yourself. Don't take graduate education as the last step towards some sort of career."

"Keep an open mind, absorb and learn, but not from just one discipline, unless you just love that one thing. Learn as much as possible in and outside of school. Absorb as much culture as you can wherever you go, whether it's in the U.S. or in a European country, absorb the cultures, learn the academics and learn everything up to whatever role you want to play."

Number two is time: Take some time to make mistakes. It's okay to make mistakes and make some detours. The Chinese education system is set up in such a way that everything is dependent on one or two things. It also decides what kind of work, what kind of prestigious job you get.

We have to absolutely abolish that kind of thinking, where students say, "Hey, I have to get into Harvard; hey, I have to get into Stanford, I have to study Computer Science because that is most in demand." I don't think that they have to worry so much about it, they have to explore, and they can afford to wait some time. Then they see that nothing is wasted. Every ounce of their experience, whether it is a detour or a straight experience taken, will actually be reflected in what they do.

Q: *The third is managing?*

A: Nope, the third is mentoring. It's finding people they actively want to emulate; it's finding people who have things they want to learn. They shouldn't struggle in the dark. Mentors can be professors, they can be coworkers, of course, they can also be parents, or people who have done a little bit of what they want to do, people who have already cleared a little bit of the path and know a little bit more of the world than they, the younger ones, do; they have the accumulation of age and experience. So the advice is also: be patient and be humble.

One of the newest social networks, Allen's company, is Babytree. This is a kind of Chinese "Facebook" for babies, small children, and their parents. Each child gets a page and parents can put up photo albums as well as receive child rearing advice. http://www.babytree.com.

Aliza Peleg, Managing Director, SAP Labs

Aliza Peleg
Managing Director, SAP Labs, U.S.[12]
Countries of Origin: South Africa/Israel
Group: The Corporate Wizards

> *"One must get involved with colleagues, have friendships outside the Israeli community: attend events, attend networking groups, industry organizations. Try as much as possible to broaden your horizons, because there is much more than was in the past, there is so much here being offered. I think the business environment here is phenomenal."*

I first met Aliza at a Forum for Women Entrepreneurs event. Aliza stuck out of the group because of her vibrant personality. I appreciated the opportunity for this interview, which gave me a closer look at her story.

Current Role

Q: *I know you work for SAP, so please tell me what position you have?*

A: I am the Managing Director of SAP Labs, U.S. First you need to understand what SAP Labs means. Especially for U.S.-based people,

12. Aliza has since left SAP Labs and is looking for new opportunities.

"Lab" has a connotation of research lab, like HP Labs, IBM Almaden Labs, Xerox PARC, on the fringes of very far-out research, with hard-core techies working on some real far-out item, which will or will not make its way to the market.

We call it a Lab, and it stands for a development location vis-à-vis sales, the go-to-market, customer engagement side of the business. That's a key differentiation; it's a full-fledged development organization and it's part of SAP's global development landscape. We have a network of eight labs around the world, and in different locations for different reasons.

The U.S. Lab is one of the bigger and more strategic labs for SAP outside Germany.

Growing up in Israel

Q: *So how did you come to do what you are doing today? How did your childhood or your family get you to the direction where you are, if at all?*

A: My family had very little influence. My parents had no influence at all, actually. They're great parents, very supportive in my journey, who exposed me to lots of stuff as I was growing up.

Q: *Where did you grow up in Israel?*

A: In Herzeliya, about 10 to 15 km north of Tel Aviv. Very nice area, where I had a great childhood, very non-pushy. Actually my parents and I, when I was a very small child, immigrated to Israel. We were originally from South Africa. My parents immigrated with four children and I was the youngest of them all. I got to Israel when I was about four years old and I had my upbringing there. My parents as immigrants didn't speak Hebrew, couldn't read or write the language. They were very "hands off." They basically said, "Kids, you're on your own."

Anti-Apartheid

Q: *What made them go to Israel?*

A: Two key factors: one is they were very Zionistic in their approach and upbringing. They really wanted to be part of the Jewish land. The other one was that they were very anti-apartheid. They didn't want to be a part of it. Many Jewish people left South Africa at that time because of anti-apartheid. Some of them went to the U.S., some went to Australia, some went to Canada. The ones who were very Zionistic went to Israel. It was a great upbringing. As for my parents' involvement in education, we were on our own.

University Studies

Q: *So what did you study and where did you go to University?*

A: I went to Tel Aviv University and majored in Math and Computer Science. Where my family may have had some influence, was in high school. I had to decide what my focus would be during the last two years of high school.

As a young girl, I was always good in the analytic and the numbers sides. I wasn't very good in the humanities, which should have lead to an obvious decision. However, making the decision to go that route was a very tough one.

Q: *As a woman?*

A: No, that didn't bother me at all. We were twenty boys and five girls in our class. That had been more or less the ratio for ten years before me, and for however many years thereafter. Both my older brothers went that route as well. And that probably made it an easier course to follow. I did worry, however, about the perception that all the geeks were in the class.

Then I also had a philosophy that I continued to embrace throughout my life based on a Hebrew saying: "I'd rather be a tail of the lions than a head on the foxes." It's sort of a literal translation. It is something which has always driven me: "Okay, they'll be smarter and better than I am, yet I'd rather be in that crowd..."

Opening the Door to Mathematics

Q: *When you went to the university, what did you do?*

A: I started off majoring in Math. Because of my experience in the youth movement and the military service, I thought to major in both Math as well as Education. I wanted to be the best high school Math teacher. I did the first year math.

At that time, you could only go into Computer Science if you graduated first year math with a very high grade. Today you can apply directly to Computer Science, but in those days, it was such a young faculty, you had to come through Math and you had to come with good grades.

Since Math was very tough the first year, I decided to start only the Math studies and leave the Education for the second year. To my greatest satisfaction, I finished the first year with good grades and that opened the door to Computer Science. I thought, "Wow, now I *have* to go," even though I had very little knowledge of what Computer Science was all about.

Q: *What year was that?*

A: I started in 1979, I finished the first year in 1980 and then I got accepted to the Computer Science faculty. Of course I'll go and take this opportunity. Then there was the same question: "Are they the cool people or are they geeks, too smart for me, whom I'll never get along with?" Needless to say, that up until today some of my best friends are from that school and they are the smartest, the greatest and the most amazing people. So I joined the Computer Science Department and got totally immersed in this world. I completely forgot about the education piece of my plan. I graduated in 1982.

Software Development/First Start-Ups

Then I started working as a software developer in Israel. I started working for a great company, a wonderful company, it was a start-up. Israel was in the very early stages of the high-tech industry. I joined a very fast moving, innovative, forward-looking company, one of the first Israeli start-ups.

Q: *What was the name?*

A: Technomatics. Up until today, it's one of the leaders in its industry, on NASDAQ, one of the very early successes of the Israeli high-tech industry. They were great people, and very strong. Many of them had come out of the Computer Units of the military intelligence. They were orders of magnitude better and smarter than I, but it was a phenomenal experience and I really loved the company. I did really well and managed to fit in. However, I did understand relatively early on, that I was not going to be a software programmer forever. I was good enough as a starter, but I probably wouldn't have been good enough for long.

Q: *And then you switched?*

A: Throughout my part-time programming job during college in a computer department of an insurance company and the work at Technomatics, I started finding other skills.

I realized I was much stronger when it came to dealing with people, interpersonal relations and connections and communication abilities. I thought I would start diverting myself, but constantly staying in the technical world.

While taking advantage of bridging the two, I started playing those roles in the company, I decided to get an MBA to complement my formal education as well as my natural skills.

Coming to the U.S.

Q: *How did you get to the United States?*

A: This is now the end of '86. My husband and I decided we would love to come to the U.S., mainly because he wanted to do his MBA. After I went through the MBA in Tel Aviv, we thought it would be much better for him to do his MBA in the U.S. He would get a much broader perspective—an outside and a market perspective. Something that would be incredibly beneficial for Israelis.

Q: *So where did he go?*

A: He went to Santa Clara University. Since I would have to support the family while he was at school, we thought the best place for me to get a job as a software developer would be in Silicon Valley. He looked at every university from San Francisco to San Jose and got accepted at a couple of schools in the area.

Six Suitcases and One Child

Q: *And you didn't have a job yet?*

A: No, we just came here with six suitcases and a two-year-old child and checked into a motel. Every morning I got up and got dressed and went for interviews. It was a good period in Silicon Valley and people were hiring. I knew one couple here in Silicon Valley...

Q: *...Americans or Israelis?*

A: Israelis. They had encouraged me, saying that for developers it would be very easy to find a job. And after a few weeks, I did. I started working and my husband started going to school. My first position was as a software developer, but relatively soon thereafter, I moved into application engineering. After a couple of years, I moved into product management. I started shifting to the other side of the spectrum, yet still in a technological field.

The first company I joined in the U.S. was a small start-up. I stayed with them for four years. Then, I went to work for Apple Computer. That's where I did the final shift, I became a Product Marketing Manager. At the end of '93, we decided to go back to Israel.

When I decided to leave Apple and go back to Israel, I was heartbroken and they were quite sorry too. I really loved the company. They decided to fund me for a year to work for Apple in Israel, to seek out technologies that were relevant to the Apple platform, either hardware or software. I had a phenomenal year. We made some real good breakthroughs. Unfortunately, it lasted only for a year. Apple started its downturn at that time.

Challenges

Q: *What are some of the biggest challenges you had to overcome in your career?*

A: You know, I don't look at it as challenges, you may have had the occasional difficulties, but overall I feel I was very fortunate. I had a very solid journey. My attitude has always been to work very hard and make the most of it.

Q: *What were the trade-offs?*

A: First and foremost, my kids—in terms of my not enjoying or benefiting as much as I could have, not having the time I could have and should have spent with them. However, it was a conscious decision from day one and it was a joint decision with my husband. To be in that kind of situation, you need to have the right husband. We overcame the challenges; we had live-ins in our home for 15 years. Many people would say, "How can you tolerate someone living in your house?"

It was obvious to me that I needed help; it was obvious to me that I'd sacrifice my privacy. It was obvious to me that my kids would be in day care.

Those were challenges. The balance was a challenge; I always felt I needed to work very hard. I was working harder not because I was a woman or because I was discriminated against. It was because I have this very demanding work ethic. Maybe it goes back to wanting to be with the herd of the lions and understanding that there are great lions around. I am very comfortable about being conscientious and accountable and working hard to keep up.

Successes

Q: *What does success mean to you?*

A: I don't want to belittle my hard work. I think I did well and I'm proud of my accomplishments. Great successes in my mind are people who created something from nothing. Amazing companies with excellent products, or services with amazing exits or financial implications. That is really what I define success as.

It's not that I don't think I am successful; I just don't want to compare my story to others'. I define success as developing a business, making the business successful, and that's an incredible achievement. The role that I have played over the past many years is much more of a back seat driver, enabling some of these amazing people, ensuring that successful concepts come to realization.

It was always amazing. Amazing people need great people behind them. And I am very comfortable being in that role.

Q: *But what does success mean to you personally?*

A: To me, success is getting up in the morning and being happy and content with first and foremost your family, your profession (where you spend 18 hours a day), and your social network around you. If you feel satisfied that you have maximized the opportunities you have in front of you, have exploited your potential to the nth degree, and you are personally, emotionally, and professionally happy with where you are—you couldn't wish for more.

Leadership

Q: *Do you think leadership has changed nowadays because we are a more global world and multicultural world?*

A: The parameters and the axis on which leaders are working have just become more complicated. I think when you talk about leadership and when you talk about having a passion and a point of view and being able to pull people along with you, that, per se, hasn't changed; but the stakeholders, the constituents are broader and more global with different needs and different perspectives. Dealing with that is a much bigger challenge.

Advice

Q: *What advice would you give Israelis who come here or who are living here, about anything?*

A: You know Israelis have been coming here since the early '80s.The Israeli high-tech industry has become embedded in Silicon Valley and vice versa. I would dare to say that there are probably 30 or 40 thousand Israelis here and that's just a rough figure, maybe even more, today.

Israel has changed so much and has matured over the past three decades, that I don't really profess to give as much advice as I would have given in my first round here in S.V.; then, most of the people were very techie. They were great engineers. They were people who didn't understand enough of the market, the business or the customer. That was true 15 years ago. Today, they are much more savvy.

Q: *So an Israeli woman who comes here and wants to be successful...?*

A: I don't see a big difference in being successful here and being successful in Israel. Of course if she is on the marketing and business side, her job will be different here than it would be in Israel. As an individual, my advice is, you have to work hard, and you have to understand what it takes to be in this game. You have to be very open-minded.

There are phenomenal people here. You have to take advantage of the diversity, maybe that's my biggest advice. In Israel we are still more or less the same types. You know all of the things, little surprises. Here, one must get involved with colleagues, have friendships outside the Israeli community: attend events, attend networking groups, industry organizations. Try as much as possible to broaden your horizons, because there is much more than there was in the past, there is so much here being offered. I think the business environment here is phenomenal.

Chi Foon Chan, President and COO, Synopsys

Chi Foon Chan
President and COO, Synopsys
Country of Origin: Taiwan
Group: The Corporate Wizards

> *"My advice is to take some risk. One key difference in Silicon Valley is that it's acceptable to fail and try again."*

I visited Chi Foon in his office and he told me many delightful stories in addition to his formal interview. He also took the time to meet my daughter and gave her career advice.

Q: *Describe what you're doing today?*

A: I'm the president and chief operating officer of Synopsys and I manage the daily operations of the company.

Childhood Experiences

Q: *How did your childhood experiences and your family influence where you are today?*

A: My family background had a lot to do with being content and always looking forward. No matter what our situation at any given time, there always seemed to be new opportunities ahead. I was born in Taiwan where my father had certain rights to gather seaweed. One day his partner just took off with their fishing boats, leaving us eventually broke. But this misfortune ended up leading us to Hong Kong where my father established a new fleet, and more adventures.

Through it all, I went to school and my family and I all learned to adapt to our changing fortune and circumstances. When I look back, I remember having a very happy childhood and a strong family.

My parents saw to it that we had an education but they never tried to force us to go in a particular direction. I've always wanted to be an engineer.

Education

Q: *Where did you get your education?*

A: I came to Rutgers in New Jersey for my undergraduate degree in Electrical Engineering. Then I got a Master's and Ph.D. in Computer Engineering—digital signal processing—at Case Western in Cleveland, Ohio. That's also where I met my wife.

Challenging Career Moves

Q: *What are some of the biggest challenges and obstacles you had to overcome?*

A: Good question—every day was a struggle [laughter]. When you look back, some things look easy while sometimes it seems like every day there were new challenges. I think I was reasonably adaptive, and most of the transitions were gradual. I can't say my whole career was planned—it was one step at a time. I worked for Intel for nine years, four years at NEC, and 17 years at Synopsys. I came to Silicon Valley in 1978, which seems like a long time ago.

Q: *How did you meet Aart [Chairman and CEO of Synopsys]?*

A: I went to NEC after Intel to manage the application team and be the General Manager of the Microprocessor Business Unit. I was at NEC for four years and I was happy in my job. Then an old friend from Intel, who was at Synopsys, called me and said, "You have to talk with this team." Aart was the founder of Synopsys and also the Vice President of Engineering and they were looking for a VP of Applications, someone who would take the product and apply it outside. Harvey Jones, who was the president at the time, also recruited me to my position.

Q: *How old were you at the time?*

A: I was 40 then and I'm 57 now. So that's how I got to Synopsys—I think I'm generally lucky in my career and in my life. I wish I could say it was all planned, but it wasn't.

Success

Q: *How do you define success?*

A: Having a good family is important to me, and being able to sleep every night is always important. But I think success is essentially a sense of knowing you're OK, that you like what you're doing and being content.

Yet that doesn't mean you're not ambitious or that you're satisfied with everything around you. I think everyone defines success differently and you tend to be friends with people who define success the same way. It's a self-fulfilling prophecy when you surround yourself with successful people. Of course, for some small groups of people, success means being able to sit around leisurely all day.

Silicon Valley—An Opportunity

Q: *Could you have become as successful outside Silicon Valley?*

A: I think Silicon Valley has certainly contributed, but it's a tough question. I always think the road not taken is one full of surprises. I think some people plan very clearly and know what they want Silicon Valley to provide and know very clearly what will contribute to their success. For me, I'm a little bit happy-go-lucky. I enjoy the journey.

U.S. Education

Q: *How did you fund your university studies in America? Did you get a scholarship?*

A: I looked at what was the lowest cost with a scholarship opportunity and it was Rutgers for my undergraduate degree. I also got a graduate fellowship, and I was lucky; by the time I was a junior, there was a good professor who came back from Sweden and didn't have many Ph.D. students yet. I was one of his undergraduate research thesis students and I received excellent attention from him. He eventually became the dean of the school.

Leadership Skills

Q: *What do you think a current leader has to know in order to be effective in the country where he or she is, and also abroad, in large companies?*

A: There are a lot of skills you need, and you have to try to quickly understand where people are coming from. Then you get deeper and deeper into the specifics.

You have to be able to grasp something and then you have to be able to integrate the input. People will talk to you, but it doesn't mean you can receive and integrate the information. Even though I'm Asian, it doesn't mean I know all the Asian ways of doing things, they are all different.

I think the first critical thing is to always understand what you want to accomplish, and setting clear objectives is essential. Of course, setting goals that are not achievable doesn't really help, and if you set goals that are sub-par, then you are not performing at your fullest potential.

I do a lot of planning in the company. I try to adjust to things. Taking responsibility is important, because things don't always go up and to the right, they sometimes go down.

Advice

Q: *What advice would you give Chinese who are living here or who are coming here?*

A: I always say, "Find [other] people who are successful, because it forces you to think about [your own] success." My other advice is to take some risk. One key difference in Silicon Valley is that it's acceptable to fail and try again.

Omid Kordestani, SVP, Google

Omid Kordestani
SVP, Google
Country of Origin: Iran
Group: The Corporate Wizards

> *"I really believe that in life you make the small decisions with your mind and the big decisions with your heart."*

A young Omid based his original ideas of this country on the sitcom "The Jeffersons"! His MBA from Stanford provided a much more updated and realistic view of the U.S.

Working at Google

Q: *Can you tell me how you describe your job?*

A: I have one of the best jobs in the world. I run Google's revenue and partnership operations, so basically anything that touches our customers and our partners and the global aspect of our business. Google is truly as global as you can get, with customers and users from Vietnam to Madison Avenue.

Family Background

Q: *How old were you when you arrived in the U.S. from Iran?*

A: I was 14. My image of the United States at the time came from the sitcom, "The Jeffersons." It was about living in Manhattan, which looked very exciting to me. One night I told my Mom, "We should move to the States." Then it was just serendipity—we had friends who were going to high school and university in the States. We arrived here and a few months later, the Iranian revolution happened.

Q: *Had your mother seen the writing on the wall?*

A: No, not at all. My mother was a nurse and my father was an engineer. We weren't into politics or anything; we were a nice middle class family in Iran.

Q: *What made her want to leave?*

A: I think it was the education part of the plan, and probably wanting to leave earlier rather than later because she felt it was easier with us being still younger; it was all timing, those are the events in life.

Q: *Where did you start out?*

A: In San Jose, California. But I consider myself very global and international.

Educational Background and Career Beginnings

Q: *So about your education?*

A: I went to high school here and then studied Electrical Engineering at San Jose State. I met a recruiter from HP at the placement office. He said, "You have this outgoing personality, you are an extrovert. Are you sure you want to be an engineer?" I said, "Absolutely." That's what you say when you're from the Middle East and have studied engineering.

However, he convinced me to consider marketing at HP. He really changed the course of my life. So I went to HP, and started to do product marketing and product management so I could travel internationally.

Q: *How old were you at the time?*

A: I was just 20.

Stanford

Q: *What made you want to go to Stanford?*

A: I took some Stanford courses in engineering over the TV at the Master's level. My passion was always engineering. But my work was all about business now and I was interested in that. I decided I really needed to get a grounding in business. HP had given me practical experience up to this point, but I decided to leave HP and reset my education at Stanford.

Confidence

Q: *Did that require a lot of confidence?*

A: I think it is shocking how much confidence you have as an immigrant. By nature you are a fighter. You come to this country to prove something to yourself, to really do the best you can in your education, the best you can in your profession; build a life and be successful. This optimism came to me through a sitcom—it's what drew me to this country. And you just believe you can't fail. I went from San Jose State to one of the best corporations in America.

Immigrants also value opportunity. That is the key part. You really cherish the fact that this country allows you to excel. I think this is probably the only country in the world that on top of the list is really your merit, what you are capable of doing, and nothing else. Maybe they notice you have an accent or they notice which state you are from or which country, but it ultimately is about what you are doing and what you represent.

Overcoming Obstacles

Q: *What have been some of your biggest obstacles?*

A: Probably the biggest one was just the adjustment of leaving my country, my friends and my family. Being uprooted was very difficult initially. The second part was financial. My mother had to work, especially after the revolution happened. She had been retired, but she had to go back into nursing and work.

Financially trying to live month to month, meeting the rent and the tuition, that was hard. Later on getting married, finances get in the way—but money was never a primary objective for me.

Q: *What about learning English?*

A: I was lucky because I went to a Catholic/Italian school in Iran, so I had studied English from the first grade on, and that was very helpful.

Google Beginnings

Q: *What made you join Google?*

A: I always had a passion to be at a start-up before it had its first funding, to be there right out of the garage stage. For me, it was this freshness about going to a start-up.

Q: *Did they recruit you, or did you know one of the founders or someone who was already working here?*

A: I knew Ram Shiram who was one of the original seed investors at Google. I had worked for him at Netscape. He introduced me to Larry and Sergei, as a way for us just to get to know each other, perhaps to help Google with its future business with Netscape. I think in the back of his mind he was also interested in my considering it. I literally wasn't thinking about it that day, but when I met Larry and Sergei, I saw the pure passion in their eyes and the karma of the place.

We actually walked back to Google on University Ave. It was the location of the company, how small it was, just a couple of offices. My life was very complicated back then, traveling all around the country, dealing with Netscape, AOL, and all those transitions. I thought, "It's so refreshing to go back and start something from the beginning."

Google Fun and Challenges

Q: *And what was the most fun and what was the most challenging in the first months?*

A: The most fun was kind of building the genesis of this organization. I knew some of the key people that I had worked with at Netscape, I asked them to join me; I tried to really get to know the two young founders there and an engineering crew that was so ambitious and so brilliant. You could tell that from day one, and I tried to bring in the business part. That was really fun. Even some of the basic things—we were like a family in those early days, we kind of ate together, we were doing street hockey, you know, we were parking the cars and watching for the Palo Alto traffic cops, because we had to keep moving the cars.

Silicon Valley Success Factor

Q: *Do you think you could have been as successful as you are now outside of the Silicon Valley?*

A: No.

Q: *Outside of the U.S.?*

A: No, not to this extent, absolutely not. Because there are all the incredible values in this country in terms of giving opportunities, the lack of prejudice, the lack of judgment about where you came from. People value you because of what you are capable of doing and what you are able to accomplish.

In Silicon Valley, the combination of the great universities, the incredible culture of innovation and entrepreneurship and the ecosystem among the universities and the venture capitalists, the attorneys, the financing structure—all of this is literally within a few miles. Sergei Brin gave a great talk at Stanford about how you can get on your bike and go talk to the lawyers on Page Mill Road and go to Sand Hill Road and talk to the venture capitalists; it's within a bike ride where you can probably hit the world's best resources for being able to start companies.

Challenges of Multicultural Leadership

Q: *What are the greatest challenges for multicultural leadership today?*

A: I think a lot of success happens through people. One of the biggest challenges is finding the right people. China is a perfect example. You have a country that is transforming itself and you have all the challenges politically and you have all the challenges setting up the business structure of the company. Ultimately it comes down to people, being able to find the right leaders, find the right employees.

Q: *What does it take on your part?*

A: It takes a lot of understanding of those cultures. You have to travel there, you have to spend time with people, and you have to spend time with potential businesses, partners, customers, government agencies. You have to be there in person. You need to respect the culture, respect the laws, be able to hire people that you can trust and who can ultimately execute with you, alongside you. The biggest challenge for me is always finding the partners, the leaders that can work with you and execute with you.

Leadership Skills

Q: *What do you think are necessary skills to be a great leader?*

A: I took a class at Stanford with John Gardner. One of the lessons I learned was that leadership can be taught. You can really learn to be a leader.

Q: *A lot of people say you can't.*

A: Exactly. And that also involves studying people back in history. Churchill is an example. War puts people into a situation where they then can become one of the most respected leaders in the world—that happened with him. You need the ability to build organizations, to build teams of people that can work with you, who respect you as a leader, but at the same time create a common mission together and pursue it together. The part that is interesting and difficult at the same time today is the fact that the world has become truly flat as Thomas Friedman has written.

The world has become more complex—as far as businesses like ours are concerned—the stage has become a global stage. To lead teams of people in multiple regions, in multiple geographies, to build leadership within your teams and set the right example, you need to hit a chord correctly.

Advice to Foreigners

Q: *What advice would you give to other foreigners, be they immigrants or not, who want to work here in the Silicon Valley or in the United States? What should or shouldn't they do?*

A: I'm obviously a big fan of coming here. I really believe this country and this region has so much to offer and so many growth opportunities. This applies even if they chose to go back to their homeland in the future.

It's an experience foreigners should have, as hard as it might be to be uprooted sometimes and to change your life. I think the core advice is this, and I hope it doesn't sound too clichè, but it really is to have the belief in yourself, and that there should really be no limit; if you have a dream—really, really believe in it and pursue it. When I look back, I am sometimes amazed and kind of scared about all those decisions I made. How could I not have applied to more than one business school—because I believed I was going to get into Stanford.

I am really a huge believer in this power of believing in your instincts and in energy; I feel the voice inside of you is really very correct.

I believe that in life you make the small decisions with your mind and the big decisions with your heart. I really believe in that. Where I have been successful is when I first did all the analysis in my head and I couldn't get to the answer. The mind always gives you the pros and cons. *But ultimately, you have to listen to your heart to make the decision and that's what works for me.*

Marc Onetto, SVP, Solectron

Marc Onetto
Executive Vice President of Worldwide Operations, Solectron[13]
Country of Origin: France
Group: The Corporate Wizards

> *"I began to feel that excitement and freedom that America brings, so I thought I could cope with the bad food."*

13. Marc Onetto is currently Senior Vice President Worldwide Operations and Customer Service at Amazon. His responsibility covers the activity of 10,000 personnel in the U.S., UK, Germany, France, Japan and China.

Marc worked for Jack Welch at GE and his contribution to GE Medical was recognized in Jack's autobiography, ***Jack: Straight from the Gut****. Jack was recently signing his new book:* ***Winning*** *at Denver University where Marc's son Philippe is a senior. Philippe showed up to have his book signed. When Philippe was introduced to Jack, he recognized the last name and asked Philippe if he was related to Marc. When Philippe said he was his son, Jack gave him a big hug in front of all his friends and told him how much he valued his Dad's contribution. A day Philippe will never forget...*

Q: *How would you describe what you are doing professionally today?*

A: I am the head of operations for Solectron. Solectron is an electronic manufacturing services company, which means we manage electronic equipment for OEMs. Our customers are all the big OEMs from Cisco to Sun to Apple to IBM, but not just here in Silicon Valley. Solectron is a global company, so we also have European or Japanese customers like NEC, Ericsson and Schneider. About 55,000 people across the world report to me in about 60 plants.

Childhood Experiences

Q: *How did your childhood experiences and family background influence your choice of careers?*

A: I guess the decision for me to come to the United States goes back many years because I came to the United States at the age of 24, as a student. I got an MBA from Carnegie Mellon University.

My Father

A: I think the original influence came from my father. When he was 20 years old, he joined the French Free Troops as a Trainee Pilot. At that time, the French Free Troops were trained in America. So he crossed the Atlantic on a liberty ship hoping that a German submarine would not sink the ship. For him, it was like going to paradise—imagine the difference from what was happening then in Europe compared to America.

He arrived as a young Frenchman wearing an American uniform with the French flag and felt very welcome. He always carried a glamorous image of America in his mind. It was a very special nine months of his life, and he often spoke of it. It must have influenced me when I was young. I guess it worked on both sides of the family, because my sister is also an executive in America.

Coming to America

The second reason for my coming to America has to do with my interest in the business world. I have a traditional French education. I was a good student in high school. So I graduated as an engineer from a *Grande École: École Centrale de Lyon*. Then I discovered that I did not have a special vocation to be an engineer and I decided that I would be a better businessman.

Business School

So that's when the idea of a business school came up, and of course America—in the mid-seventies—was the center of the world for business. So it came naturally to apply for an MBA degree in the United States. I selected a quantitative school as it was a better fit with my academic experience. That is how I arrived in Pittsburgh on the Carnegie Mellon campus in early September 1973.

The first few months in Pittsburgh were very formative times for a young man. It was my first time living outside France. I had traveled a lot in Europe. I spoke English and Spanish, but I was just a traditional French guy. Of course in the mid-70s, Pittsburgh was still the "armpit" of the U.S. It was a very tough transition compared to Paris. So I went through several steps. First there was rejection. I still remember the first day I went to the University restaurant—what a shock. I was going to have to eat this kind of "bad" food for two years! For a Frenchman this was a drama: Would I be able to survive it? But that rejection was also immediately compensated for by the academic excellence of CMU. It was an exciting place. One of my professors was Herbert Simon, the Nobel Prize winner for his work on Artificial Intelligence. There were immediate academic and intellectual challenges. I wanted to compete in terms of academic achievement with my classmates.

Anything is Doable

The other thing that I remember from my early experience was the concept that everything was doable. It was just a question of hard work, of merit, and any door would open. What a difference to "old" Europe where there are so many barriers to growth. I began to feel that excitement and freedom that America brings, so I thought I could cope with the bad food! In the second year, I made a bit of money teaching Math and Statistics. At that point I could go to one of the two decent restaurants that existed in Pittsburg at the time. Now I had the best of both worlds: good food and exciting prospects.

Perhaps the third defining moment was when I came back to France. I felt foreign in my own country! I had decided to come back to Europe as I still felt a bit alien in the U.S. because of the cultural differences.

France vs. the U.S.

I learned then that there is no place with all qualities. There is always a flip side to the qualities or there is always a flip side to the defects—and they go together. America's positive energy and openness goes with very little historical baggage. Europe's slow growth and lack of openings goes with the long history, the great cultural life, and of course the gastronomy and other elements of quality of life. You can't get one without the other. This understanding hit me when I came back to France.

Suddenly, I wasn't a Frenchman anymore, or at least not a normal Frenchman. I would see things, which felt normal before, and would now drive me crazy. My French friends would just look at me as if I were coming back from Mars. They would say, "What is wrong with you?" I suddenly realized I had a problem, that I was clearly not completely American. But at the same time, I was not a normal Frenchman any longer. I realized I had to live with this and make the best of it.

I have lived the rest of my life between America and Europe. I have been in America for good since 1992, but I have constantly dealt with the cultural gap, with the professional excitement on the American side, and the cultural quality of life in Europe. I have tried to give my children the same exposure and let them decide what they prefer between the two sides.

Challenges—The Cultural Gap

Q: *What are the biggest obstacles and challenges that you have had?*

A: I guess the number one challenge was the reason why I came back to Europe just after graduating from CMU. I didn't think I could marry an American woman. I thought the cultural gap in our daily, private life would be too much of a challenge for both sides. Now it happens that I did marry an English woman, not a French woman and perhaps this "cross channel" gap is from some perspective as wide as the French-American gap! I guess love bridges many gaps, as we are still married and we have two wonderful Anglo/Franco/American kids.

The challenge was first to establish in some form a private cocoon, where I can deal with the cultural challenge—where I can go home and I go back to a normal cultural clash between France and England rather than a more complex trans-Atlantic cultural gap. We can argue about where the center of the world is, but we'll argue between London and Paris, so it is only about 200 miles apart.

The other challenge to face is the professional career. First generation immigrants carry a strong baggage of who we are. In my case, my accent immediately marks me as different, it doesn't mean different bad or good, but it does mean different. But perhaps, more importantly, beyond the accent, there is an element of behavior that comes from your cultural background. Some elements of French behavior are perceived as arrogant, argumentative and even aggressive with many people. And beyond behavior, some of the complex interpersonal relations in the Anglo-Saxon world are sometimes still difficult for me to cope with. French social behavior is ingrained in me, despite the fact that I have been away so long and consider myself totally a citizen of the world.

Q: *The complaint from Europeans (who don't know the U.S. well) is often that the Americans are superficial.*

A: Many Europeans, especially French and Germans, have this perception of the Americans. Everybody is superficial; everybody is friendly, meaning nobody is a genuine friend. And of course, the flip side of that is that the Americans believe that the French and Germans are very unfriendly with people whom they do not know; that they are very Cartesian black and white in how they see people, and that this behavior leads to a less civil society. History tells us the Americans must be right because their society has evolved with much less drama than "old Europe" over the past three hundred years.

So we all have to recognize that we carry baggage with us, i.e., our ethnic origin; we all have our qualities and our defects and we all generate reactions from other people. When you are an immigrant in a foreign land, you have to be aware of this and learn to live with it.

Advice to Frenchmen

Q: *What advice would you give a Frenchman coming to America?*

A: I tell them to go beyond the initial rejection as fast as possible. You have to be able to go beyond your rejection and be comfortable with the good side and live with the bad side. Supporting the Green Bay Packers can be as much fun as following Marseille or Bayern Muenchen. It is quite exciting too, and once you have made the effort to understand American football rather than soccer, it is kind of fun. For the food, it is perhaps not as good in some places, but if you come to California, you will enjoy great cuisines from Asia.

The next thing I will advise them is, "Do not be worried about becoming alien to your own roots." I belong to an advisory committee to the French ambassador about improving the relationship between America and France. I have always tried to help with this. You can help both sides, and I think that is true if you are Indian or Chinese or whatever. My advice is to be boundary-less and become a citizen of both sides of the Atlantic.

What is Success?

Q: *What is success for you?*

A: The number one success is to have a fulfilling private life and a great family life. When my daughter Corinne, even at 24 years old, still comes to ask me, "What do you think about this?" That is number one, and I am very fortunate on that front.

I think the number two success, is—and there is nothing you can do about it, it comes from God or DNA—health, which is essential. Once you have these two things the rest is less important. The family success also comes with professional success. I had this discussion with my daughter one day: "Did you dislike me when you were a kid because I was never there?" And she said, "You know, it is kind of strange; of course when I was playing ice hockey in Milwaukee and you were on the other side of the world, I felt a little abandoned, but at the same time we were so proud of what you were doing, of having Jack Welch speak of you in his book."

I think professional accomplishment is part of the success in terms of your family. Certainly I was not a very good father when they were preteens. But now that they are young adults we have a great relationship. That is one thing I would define as success. Of course, with professional accomplishment comes financial success. I always joke that the real success for me will be accomplished when I will be able to make wine in Provence; not to make money but just to have my friends come and drink the wine and play petanque.

Miriam Rivera, Lawyer, Google

Miriam Rivera
Lawyer, Google[14]
Countries of Origin: Puerto Rico/U.S.
Group: The Corporate Wizards

> *"I think if you pursue things that you are interested in and you work very hard at them and you're passionate about it, you'll probably be successful IF you have selected a good environment."*

Miriam was introduced to me by my friend Walter Tijiboy, the President of Hispanic-Net. She is a fellow Stanford University alumna, and has a double degree: JD/MBA.

Q: *Tell me a little bit about what you are doing professionally today and what you have done in the last five years.*

A: Actually, I just left Google in November 2006, so I am taking a hiatus from my career, but I have been working in high tech in the Valley for the last 12 years.

Q: *Even though you are a lawyer by profession, you are in high tech. Aren't you a JD/MBA?*

A: I'm a JD/MBA and worked in high-technology law at Brobeck, Phleger and Harrison, when I first graduated. They are no longer in business. But at that time, it was a 70-year- old firm. I started out doing

---

14. Miriam has since left Google and is taking some time off.

initial public offerings, series financings, that's how I got into high technology.

I actually did a start-up with my husband, in '98; we started a company which became defunct in about 2001, during the bust.

Q: *What was it called?*

A: It was called "On Your Mind" and later "Outcome Software" and at that point we had our first child. I then went to work at Ariba and that turned out to be kind of the peak of Ariba. Within a year, they were laying off people. Even though I had been there only a year, I survived the three rounds of layoffs. I was already networking at that point given the circumstances, and then I was offered the first commercial attorney position at Google.

The Path to Google

Q: *How did you do that, was it because you knew someone, because that is how the Valley works?*

A: No, actually, it's kind of strange. I certainly had heard of Google. I had a friend whom we had laid off from our start-up; he worked at Google, and he definitely was very positive about it. But at that point, I thought I needed to go to a public company—something that could make it because my husband is working at the other one that might not make it.

So, I didn't pursue the first position that Google had, which was held then by Kulpreet Rana who is East Indian. He was the first attorney at Google. He was a patent attorney by trade and he was looking for someone to handle the commercial matters for the company. They had been looking for six months and when I met the team, including Omid [Kordestani], I thought it would be a great opportunity. It turned out to be a great opportunity for everyone.

Childhood Experiences

Q: *Tell me a little bit about your childhood background.*

A: Basically I am kind of a Horatio Alger story. I grew up in a family of five children; my parents had come from Puerto Rico to the mainland. They met each other working as migrant farm workers in Florida and they would work the crops in Florida and New York State. I was born in New York State.

My mother had a brother, who was a butcher, he got a job in Chicago. Like most immigration—it's all related to family. My parents moved to Chicago to be near my uncle and other family. My mother had a third grade education, she had been pulled out of school to kind of be the person in the family who would take care of the home, that kind of thing.

My father had graduated eighth grade. He became a lathe operator in Chicago and my mother stayed home with us for the first few years. My parents had a very bad marriage. My mother, according to her, was in a family that would now be described as "abusive" and she had picked someone to marry who was abusive. When I was nine, he left and my mother had to support all five of us on her own. She got her first job making $2,000 dollars a year just down the street from where we lived. She worked first as a receptionist at a public health clinic that we had in our neighborhood. She eventually worked her way up to become a drug abuse counselor.

Gifted Student

Then I happened to be identified as gifted in the sixth grade; I was supported by teachers to pursue private high school. I was admitted to a program called "The Better Chance Scholarship" and I went to Phillips Exeter Academy on the East Coast; I was in the second class of girls. I went in '78 and they had made it coed in '76. I went there for two years and I was doing well academically. I had high honors, but I was not culturally comfortable, it wasn't a good fit. It was like being put on another planet.

Stanford Graduate Studies

A: So I applied for a scholarship at the Latin School of Chicago from which I graduated. Then I came to Stanford and I spent about ten years off and on at Stanford doing my Bachelor's, Master's and JD/MBA.

Challenges

Q: *What were some of the biggest challenges you had to overcome?*

A: My biggest challenges? Well, definitely it's harder to be a woman in high tech than it is to be a minority, at least in my experience. Of course, I may say that because I was privileged to have the kind of pedigree that is pretty difficult for anyone to question.

When I was admitted to Exeter and was successful there, I remember one of my biggest supporters—actually the woman who had identified the ABC Program to me. There was another boy who got admitted to Deerfield Academy at the same time and she said he would be more successful than I was. I think it was a way to try to protect me. She kind of said to not set my expectations too high, and maybe that was to keep me from being disappointed.

Q: *You were saying that being a woman at Google or any high-tech company was harder—in what way?*

A: I actually think that Google is one of the better environments that a woman can work in, in Silicon Valley. I think it is more the issue that if you are working in the start-up culture, just by the nature of start-ups, they are very time intensive, they are very all-encompassing; you are supposed to spend all your time living, eating and breathing this thing. I happened to have a child by the time I was at Google, and my sense is that it was a challenge to be part of such an all-encompassing culture and such an all-encompassing success at the same time as trying to be a mother and a wife.

The men don't have the same challenges. One: all of them have stay-at home wives, they have 60 or 80 hours a week of free labor that I didn't have. I have to pay for any additional help that I have.

I'll tell you a story... we were all going as a team to the AOL offices in Virginia to work on AOL1. On that team every person had a young child. There were Omid Kordestani, David Drummond, Alan Louie, Joan Braddi and I. We were going out on the weekend, the Thursday before Easter and Joan said something that I think clinches it, she said, "I bet none of these men were up until 2:00 in the morning making Easter baskets for their kids." That's what makes it different.

We care to give our kids that kind of experience... we don't want our working to make their experiences less good. You know, you go to the Halloween store, getting all the stuff for Halloween. I think my husband is an incredible man in the sense that he is very much an equal parent with my children. That is what makes what I did possible in a lot of ways.

Success Outside Silicon Valley?

Q: *Could you have been as successful as you are now outside Silicon Valley?*

A: I certainly think this is a very special place. I think it is more than you would expect. I grew up in Chicago which is a very dynamic city, a very segregated city, and very much more openly racist.

Q: *Is it still so, you think?*

A: Less so now, but when I was growing up, it was very much a difficult environment to grow up in. I am surprised in a very pleasant way in the Bay Area by the diversity and the ability of people of color to achieve things that I do believe in many other companies across the country would just not be attainable. It definitely felt like culturally there is such a broad range of people who are working here, whether they be immigrants from Europe or Israel or Iran—it's just a very diverse and welcoming community.

Multicultural Leadership Challenges

Q: *What do you think the greatest challenges are now that we have multicultural environments?*

A: I think Google is a wonderful example of a company that appreciated the value of diversity—in large part, because its own business demanded it. In lots of companies you have to make a business case for diversity. If you are working for a company that is trying to reach the entire world, you have that built in.

That is really how my experience has been. From the beginning, we used to have a list of all the different languages spoken by our staff, so when we were doing our website, a native speaker or a fluent speaker could review it and make sure that it was idiomatic and not stiff and that it conveyed the same kind of culture that we convey in English on our site. My sense is that it was just taken for granted—that you would have this diversity.

I remember one of the first meetings I attended, I was in a room where around the table, we were discussing something of financial importance to the company. The controller of the company was an Italian immigrant, the woman who was working in the finance department on some of these matters was a Middle Eastern American, another one was an Afro-Caribbean woman, and another one was a Japanese woman finance officer from our Japan office, and I, a Puerto Rican woman. I realized that there was no truly white American male in this room. I was astounded by the diversity in the room and the fact that we were delegated the authority to make decisions on behalf of the company and none of us was white, male.

Good Leadership Skills

Q: *What three things do you think are good leadership in a company?*

A: I do think that respect for diversity is absolutely essential and the reason too, is that, in an environment that changes as quickly as the Internet and technology, you don't know what exactly you are going to need at any given moment.

The backgrounds that people bring, whether they be academically diverse, personally, ethnically or linguistically diverse, are key.

It's amazing how frequently you will be able to call on something merely because you have a diverse team. Something comes up and you can say, "Does someone know about this kind of thing, someone have some experience?" and because you have a group of people with diverse talents and backgrounds, you are so much more likely to be able to respond quickly. That was very important in our department. The other thing that I think is important, this may also be something from my Latin or immigrant culture, is how people treat others.

And you will meet one of the loveliest people, you will meet Omid Kordestani later [for an interview]. He epitomizes the kind of person who is gracious to the extreme in how he works with other people. He is a leader in my book; he is just a giant at Google. He is the kind of person who is gracious to every person he has ever worked with. He is so talented but he values other people's opinion and input. He would ask for it.

I think a lot of leaders are closed off from information because people defer to them and/or are afraid of making any waves. The person who is a leader, who thinks he knows and doesn't check, is essentially a fool, because the amount of deference that is given to high ranking people is extreme.

Qi Lu, SVP, Yahoo!

Qi Lu
SVP, Yahoo!
Country of Origin: China
Group: The Corporate Wizards

> *"I'm a believer of chance, it favors the prepared mind. If you are prepared, you perhaps are better equipped to capture and to capitalize on some of the opportunities ahead of you."*

Qi Lu and I met at 5:45 am in front of the Yahoo! complex. It was incredible to hear he sometimes gets to work at 1:00 am and is known to work until 11:00 pm.

Current Position

Q: *What are you doing now?*

A: I currently head up engineering for Yahoo!'s search business and search marketing business; with this search, we have several switch products including Web search and a collection of products we call a vertical search. I run the engineering organization for technology development mostly for those products and I'm also responsible for engineering for search marketing, which is primarily the current paid search business and contextual advertising business. So I am responsible for engineering for those businesses and products as well.

Q: *How did your childhood experiences or your family influence you?*

A: I grew up in Mainland China, in a village where in many ways I was in a disadvantaged position. I think to me this was a blessing because it taught me two things that, in retrospect, I find difficult when I try to teach them to my kids. One is motivation; you want to strive every day to be a better person, to make a difference in what you do. The second is I grew up in a place where there are fundamentally a lot of deep cultural activities and beliefs. There is a fundamental belief in knowledge and education because of 1000 years of Confucius.

Confucius' Beliefs

That carries through. Every quest for learning is doing what you do to expand the scope of human understanding. Those are the fundamental traits that perhaps I can trace back to the environment where I grew up.

I'll give you one little anecdote. I grew up in a village where, I think, there may be three hundred and fifty families sharing one school, only one teacher, just one person teaches all grades, every discipline. This teacher visits families no matter how poor the family is. When a teacher comes to your family, you borrow money or do what ever you can to treat the teacher well. So these are some of the things that are intangible and subtle. You grow up in an environment that has a profound impact on how you perceive certain things in another stage of your life.

Education

Q: *Tell a bit of your education: how did you get from your village to Silicon Valley in terms of education?*

A: In terms of education, in China it's okay. I went through primary school and middle school. In many ways I taught myself several disciplines because the teacher didn't know certain disciplines. In China, there are nationwide college entrance examinations. For the year that I went, it was in 1980, the percentage I believe nationwide was three percent of the people got accepted into college. I think I did reasonably well so I got into a college called Fudan, a university in Shanghai. I spent four years finishing my Bachelor's Degree in Computer Science and also got into graduate school. I went on to get a Master's Degree in Computer Science also in the same university and stayed on.

Q: *Why did you come to the U.S., to go to college to get some more education?*

Graduate School

A: Yes, I went to Carnegie Mellon University in Pennsylvania for my Ph.D. At that time, China's educational system did not have enough domestic expertise to offer a Ph.D. degree; the highest you could go was a Master's Degree. Again, you can say there are pros and cons, but part of Confucius' teaching is you want to go achieve excellence any way you can. You want to aim for the highest degree possible, so getting a Ph.D. is something that drove me.

If there is any opportunity, I will always go for it. Carnegie Mellon is one of the very best in terms of Computer Science. I got lucky, I got a scholarship and I could go to Carnegie Mellon.

Obstacles

Q: *What are some of the biggest obstacles you had to overcome to be where you are now?*

A: Honestly I could name some of the big obstacles, but I think perhaps I was mostly lucky to be at the right place at the right time. If anything that I can point to, it is maybe the way I grew up, having a built-in desire to strive for excellence and the willingness to work hard, to go the extra mile. Perhaps this helps me when the opportunity is there. I'm a believer of chance, it favors the prepared mind. If you are prepared, you perhaps are better equipped to capture and to capitalize on some of the opportunities ahead of you.

Long Work Hours

I was going to comment to you—when we exchanged emails, you said you didn't want to make me come at an early morning time. Actually, I usually get to work or arrive here before three o'clock in the morning. So on some days I come here at one o'clock or two o'clock in the morning, that's part of my work. I work long hours.

Q: *When do you leave?*

A: It depends; I usually leave somewhere between 10 or 11 in the evening. My work days are pretty long. To me it's important. Nobody forces me to do anything like that. I love what I do and if you get a lot of satisfaction and reward from what you do, time goes by quickly. It's not long. Every day I go to work and still feel fresh although I've been at Yahoo! for seven and a half, almost eight years.

Q: *What does success mean to you?*

A: To me it's clear, and at a certain stage it became very clear to me. It's about impact. It's about the ability to make a difference. It is actually part of the Chinese tradition, a Confucian way of teaching—when I was in graduate school, I was mostly preparing myself to be an academic and do research. The mission for me is to expand the human scope of understanding and understand things that we haven't understood before.

I feel fundamentally lucky living in this era where there are opportunities, where I get to work with wonderful people who are around me every day, and I can do things that can make a difference.

Chinese Background as an Advantage?

Q: *Did your background being Chinese give you any unique advantages at Yahoo!?*

A: I would say maybe one thing. I'm a reader. I like to read books since my job has been going from being an engineer and, over time, spending more time managing.

In one of his books, Jim Collins—he wrote *Built to Last* and *Good to Great*—has that framework of what he calls the level five leaders. The last level, the level five leader, would be a truly great level to achieve; but this doesn't mean that I am anywhere near close to this level. However, the aspiration to get there is a combination of extreme competitiveness and extreme humility; being humble, I think that comes from my country.

Listening Skills

So the way the Chinese are brought up is that it's always good to listen, it's always good to be open minded, always to be willing to accept and welcome the reality that there are always people better than you, smarter than you.

So that perhaps helps me; I think having come from an environment where you are always positioned to be collaborative and listen to other people's ideas; being supportive and open-minded is important rather than perhaps being perceived in other ways. So that's perhaps one aspect of how my Chinese background helps me.

Challenges as Multicultural Leader

Q: *So what do you think today are the greatest challenges being a multicultural leader?*

A: I haven't really thought about that, but let me just comment on what I personally believe leadership means to me. Let me see if there is anything that I think I can maybe say that relates to the multicultural nature of the workforce that we experience on a daily basis.

To me personally, I think, leadership has two aspects: one is the ability to form a vision and to articulate the direction. To me leaders are, by definition, people whom others will follow.

So it's not because of the position in the company you have, but it is really about the ability to say, "We are going to head that way, this is what the future looks like." That's one. The second is to be able to have the skills, the power of persuasion to mobilize the resources, to go along with them. If you're only capable of articulating the vision and direction, but without the necessary capabilities of getting to the point whereby the company or whatever organization you're trying to lead can go along with that, then you don't have good leadership.

You need both the capabilities of saying where you're going and then getting there. I think to me, these two are a combination of very important, fundamental traits and qualities of leadership.

Advice

Q: *What advice would you give to Chinese who are either living here or coming to work here?*

A: For me I would say, go with your passion and have the willingness to perpetuate excellence for learning. Excellence is always good to have, and if there are opportunities to find people who can mentor you, that also helps.

Future China/India Growth

Q: *How do you see China and India growing economically and also in terms of knowledge, in the next years?*

A: Perhaps one of the advantages of being ethnical [*sic*] Chinese is that I do understand their markets better; I have language and cultural advantages. I've been to India once; we have a workforce in Bangalore. And the workforce is an offshore India team we've had for about four or five years. It's fascinating to me when I interview people there and hire them and work with them.

I learned a lot about myself by working with the offshore team in India. In China, I participated in a lot of business dealings. I went back to China five times last year alone, so my personal view is: there are just tremendous amounts of opportunities in terms of economic growth in these two countries, China and India. In China, I would say the amount of investment, the amount of technological investment, the pace of change... You go there three months later and a lot of things have changed; in another couple of months, things change again. I personally think there are opportunities there for people who have career aspirations, particularly for those who want to make a difference.

Future Opportunities

I could say the same for India. For me personally, this is one of those things that I would like to do—I would like to go back to China to work out something, maybe work with some of my friends. Education is the area that I have a passion for because I taught at the university and there are different ways doing education, different ways of doing research, and there are just tons of opportunities ahead of us.

Shantanu Narayen, President and COO, Adobe Systems

Shantanu Narayen
President and Chief Operating Officer, Adobe Systems[15]
Country of Origin: India
Group: The Corporate Wizards

> *"Focus on the task at hand and the fruits will take care of themselves."*

Shantanu received me in his beautiful office at Adobe. He is an accomplished and educated businessman who survived his time as a student in the Midwest even while being a practicing vegetarian.

Q: *What do you do at Adobe?*

A: My role here at Adobe is to focus on strategy, to make sure that we build a great team and execute against that vision. My title is President and Chief Operating Officer.

---

15. As of November, 2007, Shantanu Narayen was appointed CEO of Adobe Systems.

Childhood Experiences

Q: *How do you think your childhood experiences and your family influenced where you are today?*

A: I grew up in a city called Hyderabad in India. My father ran his own business after studying in the States and working in the States and the Middle East. My mother was a professor, ironically, of American literature; she worked at Osmania University. So I came from a family where there was a lot of focus and emphasis on education.

My father studied in the States, worked here for a few years and then went back. My brother followed in his footsteps as an engineer and I was expected to do the same. Growing up in India in those days, you were expected to study either engineering or medicine, and in India a lot of people tend to follow the profession their parents have. I think it has changed dramatically over the last 20 years, but that was the case then. My mother wanted me to be a doctor, my father, an engineer. The sight of blood made me squeamish, so it was a pretty easy choice.

Educational Path

Q: *What was your educational background?*

A: I did my engineering at Osmania University in Hyderabad, where I grew up. I studied Electrical Engineering. It was really the precursor to Computer Science when I studied in those days.

Q: *Did you like it?*

A: There were two parts to Electrical Engineering: "power engineering," which is what my father studied, and "circuits" which was pre-Computer Science. I hated power engineering. I absolutely hated it. It was in the last few semesters that I studied Computer Science and programming. That was a lot more fun.

It was Fortran and assembly language. There were no personal computers; you had to actually submit a job. Having to submit jobs forced you to debug your programs in parallel. I don't think it was all bad. But I actually wanted to come to the States to do an MBA.

Focus on Graduate School

Q: *Where did you want to go?*

A: Well, at that point an MBA wasn't an option, since you could not receive financial assistance, so I didn't even apply. I applied for a Master's in Computer Science at multiple universities. I applied to Austin, [Texas] where my brother went, I applied to UC Berkeley, and I applied to a whole bunch of schools. The only school that gave me financial assistance was a small school in Ohio, called Bowling Green State University, so I went there. It was the best decision I ever made in my life, because I met my wife there.

I went to Bowling Green for two years. My brother had already come to California, so as soon as I graduated, I came to California and I found a job here. I worked at Apple for many years and finally did go back to get the business degree that I always wanted at Berkeley, but part time.

Q: *Did the food bother you? Some of the French executives that I've been interviewing say, "Oh my God, the food was terrible."*

A: I am a vegetarian, so the choice in the Midwest was very limited. I mean steak was considered vegetarian [laughter]. The whole notion of not eating anything that had meat in it wasn't really possible. So that was the first time I started to cook, and I had never cooked in my life before. You learn fast. It's funny because I roomed with two other Indian people; one would clean, one would cook, one would have the day off. We had that rotational assignment.

Career Challenges

Q: *What were some of the biggest challenges you had to overcome in your career?*

A: I have been pretty fortunate, I must confess. Growing up in India, especially doing engineering, was challenging. I apprenticed for a newspaper in India growing up and I really wanted to be a journalist, but journalism was not considered a "choice career." Academics were the furthest thing from my mind as a high school senior.

Then I came to the States, and I have been very fortunate. The six degrees of separation among the Indian community is pretty good, and my first job I got through a friend of my brother at Apple. I was interviewing with a whole bunch of companies, but it's always been networking that's really enabled me to find my next career move.

Success

Q: *What does it mean for you to be successful?*

A: Well, I will give you two answers. The more important one for me is personal success, which is all about my kids. I have two kids and we're raising them to be good people and equipping them to do well. That's probably the biggest success for me right now.

In business, it is the ability to truly have an impact. It doesn't have to be a profound impact. If it is by association with Adobe, I can say we have helped change the world, which I do believe we have.

Teams that Work

The other thing I would say, as a manager, is that you define your success by the success of your team. If your team is successful, chances are you will be very successful as well. You have to clarify what the hill is that you are trying to conquer, and how you get there, because people like to do that. It's removing obstacles and offering guidance and advice. It's less about managing them directly day-to-day at this level.

Indian Background

Q: *Does your background as an Indian give you any unique advantages in business?*

A: It is a global society, and if there is one thing I might have an edge on, it's sensitivity to cultures and how different people react. Then again, I was fortunate to live in a household where people were exposed to the U.S. My ability to assimilate in this country was perhaps made easier for me than for other immigrants who might come, because there was so much exposure to the culture, the language, the literature while growing up. I think a number of first-generation immigrants are very driven, because failure is not an option.

Challenges for Leadership

Q: *What do you think are the greatest challenges for multicultural leadership today?*

A: Well, one of the biggest challenges to leadership is that it is so easy to believe that everybody has the same DNA and to treat them all the same as opposed to really understanding what motivates people and how they would like to be treated.

U.S./India/China—An Economic Comparison

Q: *Who is going to win economically, China, India or America?*

A: I look at it this way, what are the key elements of the three places?

America has been incredibly successful because of the higher education system and the investments that previous governments made in the Internet and DARPA.

A lot of the progress came from really far-sighted individuals who believed in investing in infrastructure. The immigrant population in the U.S., I think, has also contributed significantly to the success of America. It is the most open society of the world, and as long as those things continue to be what the U.S. stands for—an openness, a willingness to accept new ideas and a focus on the future—those will be the success factors for the U.S.

One of the big differences I see between India and China is that China has the ability to invest in massive infrastructure projects, given that the government has the ability to mandate a whole bunch of things, and that allows a certain amount of rapid progress. That unfortunately takes a little bit longer in India, in a democracy. I went to this software center in Beijing once, and eighteen months prior it had been a residential area. So if there is foresight by the people who are managing that kind of change, all this is possible at a much quicker pace than in a democratic process.

Q: *And in India?*

A: I think the language is a huge success factor and, overall, the fact that there is a democracy, that there is a judicial system, and that there is a very large intelligentsia that has now savored the fruits of an open economy in a society. I go back to India nowadays, and their confidence that the world is their oyster is very refreshing.

Even in my generation, the transformation really hadn't started, so it is refreshing to see these people believe that there is no end to what they can accomplish. It's going to be amazing. Hopefully each country will find what is working well in other countries and maybe incorporate it into their own.

Advice to Indians

Q: *What advice would you give Indians who are living here or coming here to do well?*

A: Be yourself and don't try to be something you are not. There is a tendency to want to fit in or stand out. You have to really be true to yourself. People who are successful, at the end of the day, they know what they want to accomplish.

There is a saying in the Bhagavad Gita, which translated is, "Focus on the task at hand and the fruits will take care of themselves." That has always guided my philosophy. Do what you are supposed to do and good things will happen, and they have.

Sarit Firon, CFO, Olive Software

Sarit Firon
CFO, Olive Software
Country of Origin: Israel
Group: The Corporate Wizards

> *"At the end of the day, people evaluate you as a woman on the basis of your talent, professionalism and personality."*

Sarit is an incredibly smart and vivacious executive. She knows what it takes to balance work and family life. She was eight months pregnant when she helped negotiate the $200 million sale of P-Cube.

Q: *What are you doing now?*

A: I am the CFO at a software company, Olive Software. I joined them a year ago.

Childhood

Q: *How do you think your childhood led you to what you are doing now?*

A: I was born in Israel and lived in a small city close to Tel-Aviv. Neither of my parents has a formal education, nor, in fact, did they finish high school. They immigrated from Hungary and Egypt to Israel and when they were kids; their families were quite poor and didn't have the means to provide them with a good education. Despite their background, however, they valued higher education a lot and wanted us kids to have a better future. From the very beginning, I remember, at home, they spoke about the importance of school and then university.

University Studies

Q: *What did you study at the university?*

A: I studied Economics and Accounting at Tel Aviv University, which is a top university in Israel. In order to enroll in a good university in Israel, it's not a matter of money; it's a matter of grades.

Challenges

Q: *What were the greatest challenges that you faced, and how did you come to the United States?*

A: The greatest challenge was the financial side for me. When I finished the army service, I was 21 and I didn't have any money at all. My parents couldn't afford to pay for the university. I had to work in order to finance myself and at the same time to learn. Most of my friends went on a big trip abroad but I devoted the first year after the army only to work in order to save money. During my studies, I had to work and clean houses. Work interfered significantly with my studies and I had to miss many classes. But I was lucky, because university was pretty easy for me, I finished it in three years.

Coming to the U.S.

Q: *What brought you to the United States?*

A: After the university, I started to work as a CPA and then as a controller and CFO. My first role as a CFO was for RADCOM, a private company which went public on NASDAQ during my tenure.

After five years at RADCOM, a friend of mine told me about P-Cube. P-Cube seemed to be very interesting, but I thought it was a too early stage company for me.

However, it turned out that P-Cube intended to open its headquarters in Silicon Valley and offered to relocate me, including my family. This was a whole different proposition for me as it was an old dream for my husband and me to spend a few years in the U.S.

Working in High Tech as a Woman

Q: *As a woman, what has it been like working in the high-tech industry?*

A: There are some advantages but also disadvantages. First of all, at the end of the day, people evaluate you as a woman on the basis of your talent, professionalism and personality. Occasionally I could feel that people who didn't know me had the attitude of, "She is a young woman, looks nice, probably not smart enough," that changed later to, "Oh, she knows what she is talking about." I believe that this attitude made me act more assertively on purpose. In terms of compensation, I think that I was always paid fairly like men, but I think that I had to work harder to convince people that I deserved it.

I cannot exactly define the advantages of being a woman, as it is very intangible; it is more of a feeling that sometimes—whether in an argument, negotiation, or any other interactive business with men—it seems to me that being a woman plays a positive role.

What is Your Definition of Success?

Q: *How do you define success?*

A: Success for me is first and foremost having a happy family and a fulfilling life. I have a great family: a husband and three daughters and I was lucky to have such a family while not giving up fulfilling myself. Despite my career, I was (and stayed) a very family-oriented person and my career could never fulfill me the way my family does.

My career started as a means to provide us with the financial strength to achieve some other goals, but along the way, I understood that it wasn't just a means, but rather it was my way to fulfill my intellectual needs, stay intrigued and enjoy day-to-day life. I was probably the youngest, very successful CFO for a certain number of years. I had a diversified career in public and private companies; all of them were successful. I felt good and it was a boost for my self-esteem, which is also a kind of success for me.

I think that many people refer to financial success when they describe someone as successful, but I felt successful long before I was financially successful.

Leadership Traits

Q: *What are the three traits a leader should have and three traits a leader should not have?*

A: A strong personality, being smart and self-confident, these are very important qualities. He or she should also be very flexible, be able to work in a very good and efficient way when being under a lot of pressure and in an uncertain environment.

A leader should never treat people rudely or arrogantly. Good personal skills are very important. Personally I think that honesty is very important, a leader should not act dishonestly.

Advice

Q: *What advice would you give to Israelis coming here?*

A: I think it is important not to change who you are but try to get to know your colleagues' habits and show them respect. They will respect yours in return. In your profession, try to learn the new aspects that relate to the U.S. as fast as you can, and don't try to force practices that are common in Israel. Try to adopt new ones that are more suitable or adjust yours so they will fit. Also, remember to get involved socially and professionally with people other than Israelis. And lastly, work hard and keep high standards. It always pays off, no matter where you came from.

Chapter 7

The CEOs

It takes a certain type of person to rise to the position of CEO. Great CEOs are great leaders. They know themselves and what they stand for. No matter how tough it is to start the company, it's even harder to keep it going and growing. Their reputation depends on making countless tough decisions every day and being comfortable with the exercise of power. They must answer to customers, employees and investors.

It's no surprise that in an era of tough competition among global corporations, many successful CEOs have global experience. To this extent, foreign-born CEOs have a built-in advantage. They overcame whatever obstacles they needed to in order to succeed early in their career. This included relocating from their home country to the U.S. and becoming effective businesspeople in America. Their trajectory is often faster and higher than American-born executives because they are the exception that proves the rule. Listen to the stories of the CEOs.

- Aart de Geus, Chairman and CEO, Synopsys
- Marylene Delbourg-Delphis, Interim CEO

- Philippe Courtot, Chairman and CEO, Qualys
- Guy Gecht, Chairman and CEO, EFI
- Dan Maydan, CEO Emeritus, Applied Materials

Aart de Geus, Chairman and CEO, Synopsys

Aart de Geus
Chairman and CEO, Synopsys
Countries of Origin: Netherlands/Switzerland
Group: The CEOs

> *"For me hell is boredom. If there is one thing I cannot handle, it's boredom."*

Aart de Geus is one of the recognized leaders of his industry. His schedule sometimes makes it difficult to find time on his calendar. I was fortunate he squeezed me into a 30-minute slot he happened to have open.

Running a Company

Q: *Describe what you are doing today as CEO of Synopsys. What does that involve?*

A: I run a billion-dollar-plus, high-tech company, so it involves everything: planning, execution, Wall Street, customers, employees. There is no angle of the company that is foreign to me. Having founded it, I've seen it grow in all dimensions. Aside from my family and a little bit of a personal life, this position is all-encompassing.

Q: *How long have you been here in the U.S.?*

A: Since 1979.

Q: *What is your overseas background, including education?*

A: I'm an Electrical Engineer by training. I grew up in Europe. I was born in the Netherlands, but grew up mostly in Switzerland. Part of that time was along Lake Geneva in Vevey, which is French-speaking. I went to Lausanne for the Polytechnical Institute, but I spent my adolescence in Basel, in the German-speaking part of Switzerland. Then I came to the U.S. to get a Ph.D. in Electrical Engineering from SMU in Dallas.

Childhood Influences

Q: *What influence did your childhood and your family have on where you are today?*

A: I felt a definite push from my family to get a good education, as well as to be open to the world beyond our borders. The very fact that my parents immigrated to Switzerland in the late '50s was an example of that, and quite uncommon at the time.

My father found a job at Nestle in Vevey, and he didn't hesitate to move us from the Netherlands. For him, it was simply a mental expansion of possibilities. In many ways, my immigration to the United States was on the same scale as what my parents did.

Q: *And they stayed there?*

A: Yes, my close family is still in Switzerland.

Q: *What made you leave?*

A: Mostly, a desire for change. I wanted to try something different. I am not quite sure why I ultimately chose North America. I first tried for Canada, but ended up in the U.S. I wanted to go abroad to graduate school. It was a good way to *get away from* the familiar, not necessarily *to go toward* something clear-cut in my mind.

First Job while at Graduate School

Q: *What did you do after SMU?*

A: Actually, even *during* SMU, I joined General Electric. That was partly due to my advisor. He had joined GE and decided to coach me from there on my Ph.D. thesis. So I ended up working on my Ph.D. thesis at night after working at GE all day—which is not an ideal game plan, by the way. But somehow it all worked out. So I worked for General Electric in North Carolina for about five years.

Founding a Company in the Eighties

Q: *Where did you find the drive to found a company?*

A: There was a lot of luck involved, or you can call it circumstances and timing. In a nutshell, we had some breakthrough technology, there was a need for change in the way engineers were designing chips, we ran into some venture capitalists, and voila! Suddenly, almost out of nowhere, came this idea: "Could we start this company?" And we did.

Motivation

Q: *Was it fun?*

A: "Fun" is a complicated word. On one hand, it was fun; but I would say it was more "high intensity" than anything else. It's been 20 years now at high intensity, which must be fun; otherwise, I wouldn't keep doing it.

But deep down, the motivation is more than a search for fun. What's more motivating to me is the opportunity for never-ending learning. The reason I don't like the word "fun" so much is because too many people associate it with, "Oh, things are going really well." But it's more than that.

It's certainly not "fun." I think it is intensity, commitment and the drive for success.

In any event, all of that certainly beats boredom. Someone once said, "Hell is whatever you like to do most in life, but you have to do it all the time." For me hell is boredom. If there is one thing I cannot handle, it's boredom.

Obstacles

Q: *What were some of the obstacles that you had to overcome?*

A: Well, in some ways, everything is an obstacle when you haven't experienced it before. Here's an analogy: Many people think, "I sort of know what it is like to fly on the Space Shuttle; you see these guys on TV, floating in space." But I think actually being *on* the Shuttle is quite different from that. Likewise, many people think, "Oh, I sort of know what running a company must be like," but you truly have no idea until you are in the midst of it.

Challenges

Q: *What challenges have you had to overcome, in your leadership role?*

A: It may sound a bit like a cliché, but I think you have to welcome every challenge as an opportunity. Once you do that, the actual particulars of the challenge don't matter so much. If cleaning the windows grows our business, I clean the windows. As a matter of fact, I did just that at our first office!

But that's just a hint of what you must be willing to do. An entrepreneur is someone who makes things happen. What the "things" are is subject to the circumstances. If your visitor wants black coffee, you make sure you have black coffee. If your visitor wants a very high-quality product, you'd better have a very high-quality presentation.

Success Lives on Two Levels: Corporate and Personal

Q: *How do you define success?*

A: I think there is a corporate level of success and a personal level. For the corporate level, you have three main constituencies, and maybe a fourth.

The major constituency, number one, has to be your customer. That's the party you make a commitment to deliver something to, and they pay you for it.

The second constituency is the employees. That's the team. Loyalty to your team, a commitment to investing in mutual growth, and support are vital—including through some of the down cycles, including the personal down cycles of people's lives.

The third constituency has to be the investors—public or private. They are actually less loyal than either of the other two constituencies, but you have sort of a contract, which is that they are your *de facto* employer.

You could add a fourth constituency, the surrounding community; but from a business point of view, that's less contractual. However, I have always tried to do things for the communities that have provided a friendly environment for our business.

On the personal level, personal success is different for everyone. For me it's very clear. It's two things: one is never-ending learning; and two, the interaction with people I like, that I care about, and that are stimulating, which goes back again to learning.

Life in or outside the Valley?

Q: *Do you think you could have been just as successful outside Silicon Valley? Or is this environment really the only place where you could grow and where your ideas could be fertilized?*

A: There's no question that I could have learned as much in other places in the world. There is also no question that I could have interacted with very stimulating people in other places in the world. Built a great company? I probably could have done that in other places as well.

But could Synopsys have grown as fast or made as much impact elsewhere? I doubt it. The environment here is much more conducive to rapid incubation, growth, and leverage of high-tech companies. So at least one element is specific to Silicon Valley.

Background as a European

Q: *Does your background as a European give you any unique advantage as a CEO?*

A: Well, at a minimum, it gives me the advantage of being able to see the world from two perspectives—the perspective of living here and of having lived there. There is an advantage to having grown up with multiple languages, too, and I have always argued that languages are cultural windows.

Global Challenges

Q: *What are the greatest challenges globally today for leaders; or does it make any difference if it's global or if it's local?*

A: I think there are practical characteristics as well as cultural characteristics.

From a very practical point of view, the most important thing is that you have to be able to survive jet lag. Let's face it: If you are a global leader and if you have to travel a lot, like I do, my biggest enemy is jet lag. At least a quarter of my life is spent at less than optimum performance, just because I have to survive a pretty big challenge to my body.

From a cultural point of view, you have to have some degree of openness or, at least, an understanding that different cultures may have different perspectives, that they may have different ways of doing things. There may be different speeds of doing things, too. At a micro level, tech support in the Deep South won't necessarily respond as quickly as they do in Silicon Valley. Likewise, phrases that are trivial in the U.S. may be a big deal if you say them in another country. It is rather baffling to see some of the political leadership in the United States having no clue about some of those things.

Good Leadership

Q: *What should good leaders have to be able to work well with employees?*

A: At least three qualities are must-haves:

First, I have always felt that at the heart of any form of leadership, there must be some degree of integrity about what one stands for.

We translate it at Synopsys into, "Do what you say and say what you do." It's a simple, to-the-point definition of integrity.

I have found over and over again that the success of an organization is directly linked to the strength of its values. Those values come out especially during any downturns.

When things go well, everybody is best friends, so it's easy to be a great leader. It's when things get tough that people stick with it because they actually share values. It makes a huge difference on the group's efficiency as well. If you feel the same way I do about how important it is to support a customer, there is no debate; we know what we need to do. But if part of the group thinks, "To heck with the customer; that's not my biggest priority right now," you become inefficient as a group. Some degree of values and integrity is at the heart of every success story.

Second, leading implies that somewhere, somebody else is following. People follow only if the leader creates a vision that motivates others to move. That vision can be for a business or for personal growth. People who feel they have an opportunity to grow are very, very motivated. People who feel that they can have an impact—that is extremely motivating.

Leading is a combination of setting a vision, a direction, and getting people to buy into it with their heart and soul.

Third, leading implies successful execution, which requires management. Management is very much the meat and potatoes, the nuts and bolts of how you make a business run, the processes that you put in place to keep a group running in the same direction.

Which Culture Dominates?

Q: *I have always wondered: is corporate culture more important than personal country culture? Is there a Synopsys culture, even though you may have 20 different cultures working for you—Indians, Chinese, Germans, French, etc.?*

A: There is absolutely a corporate culture. And, in fact, the corporate culture actually decides who else becomes part of the corporate culture. If you interview someone and they come across as somebody who is not going to fit, they won't make it into the company; therefore, they won't change the corporate culture.

As much as we believe, on one hand, it is really good to bring in new people—and don't get me wrong; diversity is always a strength—it is also true that if people don't fit because of their values, they will get ejected by the system. And a good system makes sure of that.

Music

Q: *What do you do in your spare time?*

A: I play electric blues guitar in pick-up bands. Give me a key, give me the tempo, and off we go...

Marylene Delbourg-Delphis, Interim CEO

Marylene Delbourg-Delphis
Interim CEO
Country of Origin: France
Group: The CEOs

> *"The art of learning is to forget what you know and assume that you don't know everything. This appears to be an obstacle for the French people when they arrive. Usually they have a very good academic background, but they may be somewhat dogmatic."*

Marylene has many roles: a turnaround CEO, a Doctor of Philosophy, a journalist, and is the author of several books on the history of fashion and fragrance.

Q: *What are you doing today?*

A: As a consulting, interim or turnaround CEO, I help companies create and define their offering, build their strategy, and structure their operations.

Childhood Experiences

Q: *Tell me a little bit about your upbringing and where this has led you.*

A: My parents were both teachers and when I was a child, I thought I would be a teacher as well. My parents loved teaching and it was just something that was natural for me.

Adieu Philosophie

After I graduated from *l'École Normale Supérieure*, I started to teach philosophy. I was destined to climb the ladder within the French University system... until I wondered if this was really what I wanted to do.

Q: *What triggered the change?*

A: I loved and still love philosophy. I loved teaching. Yet, I had the feeling that I was missing something, the real world. In a way, when you study philosophy, you have the feeling that you know everything without having seen anything.

So I decided to become a journalist, to provide myself with this supplemental experience. I went to *Le Monde* and, of course, they thought that I wanted to join one of their political departments, as there would have been some continuity with my background. They were somewhat shocked when I said that I wanted to write on the fashion and fragrance industry.

At first, they didn't take me very seriously. At the end of the seventies, it was not fashionable for intellectuals to like fashion. It had been in the '40s and '50s and a little bit in the '60s and definitely not at the end of the '70s.

Goodbye to Journalism

Q: *How does this take us to the computer industry?*

A: As I was writing on the perfumery industry for *Elle*, I went to Saint Gobain, which was a main producer of perfume bottles. They had started a small database on the history of perfumes on the Apple II and asked me if I wanted to help them. The small custom file manager they were using was not sufficient. To make a long story short, I ended up creating a database company in 1984 that would be able to not only manage my research on perfumes, but also manage any type of data.

Q: *Another big jump! You are working on perfumes and then you create a database company.*

A: I loved computers the minute I discovered them. The mid-eighties were exciting times. Macintosh had come out and everything seemed possible—all the more so as data management on the desktop was in its infancy. So I contracted a programmer to build the first relational database—and graphical database—on a microcomputer. Eventually the program was to be called 4th Dimension and became a best-selling product.

Managing Bootstrapping

Q: *What happened to your research in philosophy, your work on the fashion and the fragrance industry?*

A: I had to choose. I didn't have time for what had been my previous life. Managing a bootstrapped company that grew reasonably quickly once the product was finalized, and after that creating the U.S. subsidiary in 1987, it required my undivided attention. Or rather, almost undivided, because I had a daughter, Sophie, in 1988.

Q: *How was it to be a woman starting a company in the eighties?*

A: I was so committed to what I was doing that I downright discarded the snide remarks of the skeptics. It is true that I had everything going against me. I was one of the rare women in a male-dominated field. My background was not in business. I had selected a computer which did not have a business image, with a small market. I kept in mind the encouraging remarks of people whom I respected, among them Jean-Louis Gassée and Alain Rossmann.

Given that I was working all the time, I could not create a large network. After the fact, because they were not nearly as famous as they are today, I feel that I had pretty good taste in the selection of my mentors. Also, I hired the right person to run the U.S. subsidiary during the first two years, from 1987 to 1989: Guy Kawasaki. He was the Apple evangelist at the time, and I will always be grateful that he accepted to work for a woman—and a French woman at that.

Q: *Was this his first entrepreneurship experience?*

A: Yes. I think that the combination of the skills he developed at Apple as an evangelist and what he learned in a bootstrapped company built a phenomenal basis for what his career is now. All his books on entrepreneurship ring true. I can only advise entrepreneurs to go listen to him and read his books.

Permanent Move to the U.S.

Q: *What came next?*

A: At the end of 1993, I left my own company and settled permanently in the United States. Since then, I have helped a significant number of companies. More recently, I was the CEO of a great company, Brixlogic, focusing on the implementation of industry standards for the financial and insurance industry, and a major player acquired it.

Biggest Obstacles?

Q: *What were the biggest obstacles you had to overcome if you were to name three?*

A: After the fact, I see only one, being a French woman, i.e., French and a woman.

Q: *Which was harder?*

A: In the past, probably both. When you are French, you had and still have to overcome the obstacle of being perceived as arrogant. On top of that, being a woman added a second kind of liability. The Silicon Valley was not as open as it is today, even in the early '90s. Things are easier now, American entrepreneurs may sometimes wonder when they are advised to give me a call by a VC or another entrepreneur, but my resume is my best advocate.

Advice

Q: *Last question: what advice would you give a French woman or a French man coming to or living in Silicon Valley to be better in business, maybe to adjust better?*

A: To learn how to listen. The art of learning is to forget what you know and assume that you don't know everything. This appears to be an obstacle for the French people when they arrive. Usually they have a very good academic background, but they may be somewhat dogmatic. This can be true also for other countries. If you want to do something in a country, you have to stop thinking, "Well, in France, we do this, and here in the U.S., you do that." The minute you forget about "we do"-"you do," you understand what living in another country is. So, stop making comparisons. Work and play by the rules.

Philippe Courtot, Chairman and CEO, Qualys

Philippe Courtot
Chairman and CEO, Qualys
Country of Origin: France
Group: The CEOs

> *"The strength of the American system, as it continues to absorb immigrants, is adaptability. One could say that the European lifestyle is more evolved compared to America, but when you spend all your energy protecting what you have, you cannot evolve."*

Philippe Courtot is one of the pioneers of the IT industry. He has repeatedly turned innovative companies into industry leaders; his main focus is on customer satisfaction and investor value.

Current Position

Q: *How would you describe what you are doing professionally today?*

A: I've got two roles in Qualys. One is to make sure that the information in the company flows everywhere, so that everybody is aware of everything, and the other is, to make sure that everybody understands the real needs of our customers.

World as a Global Market Place

Q: *You have operations outside the U.S.; does that mean information flows everywhere?*

A: The world is becoming a global place; information has to flow everywhere, without friction, both inside and outside of the company with our partners, customers, outsourcers, with the media, the influencers.

As competition is becoming more global, as the Internet flattens distribution, as product cycles shorten and as customers have a greater ability to "switch," it has become paramount that individuals in every company work together with the interest of the customer at heart, rather than with their sole interest or only the interest of the company. It is a very different focus than the one learned in an MBA school.

Scientific Approach

Q: *How did you come to be doing what you're doing today?*

A: You know what has always driven me was trying to understand things with a scientific approach; I studied physics and I am still fascinated by how much and little we really know. I could not really find a job as a physicist at the time and decided to get into computers instead while I lived in France in my late twenties.

Q: *In terms of jobs, what did you do?*

A: I founded the French subsidiary of a computer company called Modular Computer Systems, Modcomp, and then I became in charge of that in Europe. But I really wanted to go to the U.S. because I realized very early on that working in France was quite limiting as I was not from the "elite," therefore working for an American company was much more promising. One could see most of the French management came from the same schools [les Grandes Écoles], that they were a caste, and that if you were not part of them, it would be hard for you to climb the ladder—and, they were also quick at making you aware of it.

Coming to the U.S.

Q: *So how did you come over here to the United States?*

A: I had decided to immigrate to the U.S. I started the French subsidiary with $5,000 and then was promoted two years later to run Sales and Marketing for Europe, based in London. Then I came to the U.S. in 1981 to run International and finally ended up as Head of Marketing worldwide.

Q: *Where were you located in the U.S.?*

A: Modcomp was based in Fort Lauderdale, Florida, and I was living in Boca Raton, Florida. After that, I was recruited by Thomson-CGR in the U.S. to be the President of Thomson-CGR, U.S. In less than two years, we made the company profitable by focusing on the mammography market and grew our market share in mammography from 2 percent to 40 percent in 24 months, competing against GE, Siemens and Philips.

Q: *What part did you play in that growth?*

A: I had to fight the French management as they didn't want us to go into mammography because that was not their plan, it was not their view.

So they told me many times, "Philippe, we are the ones devising the strategy, not you; and you should do what you're told to do." What they wanted, because they had subsidies from the French Government, was for me to penetrate the U.S. market for MRIs. In reality, I could not see how this could be done, but they would not hear it, as what they wanted us to do at that time was to promote the magnetic resonance units. So I found a way to focus resources on the mammography market, and what was very telling was that rather than rewarding me, like any American company would have done, they reprimanded me for not having followed their instructions.

Marketing Focused

Q: *But tell me—if your background was in physics—where did you get that flair for marketing?*

C: I think it's that desire of trying to understand the fabric of the universe that I channeled and that differentiated me from a lot of marketers, and MBAs particularly, who are taught a recipe for success. Simply, I was and always will be genuinely trying to understand the customer, the market, the product, the competition—not what they do poorly but what they do well. Always trying to understand the real reasons behind such things as: why would people want to do that? Why do they need to do that?

The other component is the intellectual honesty physicists have to have or develop—the facts are the facts and no matter what they say, you have to accept them. I also believe that I am a creative and artistic person and I blended this with my quest for understanding.

Q: *So after Thomson's, where did you go?*

A: Thomson-CGR was acquired by GE, thanks in great part to our big success in mammography. Venture capitalists in the Silicon Valley (the turnaround team of H&Q), who had invested in a medical company had noticed what we did at Thomson and recruited me. I arrived in '87 in the Valley to help them rejuvenate Adac Labs. There, I learned how efficient turnaround experts can be, but I was unhappy.

They were far too interested in the short term results so they could flip their investment, as they had put new money from their turnaround fund, namely the Phoenix fund, into the company which had collapsed and were expecting quicker returns. They were in fact re-investing in such companies at 10 cents on the dollar and the objective was to re-sell that investment a year later at 40 cents on the dollar.

Early Email Application

I wanted to go back into the computer field. So I looked around in the Valley and found ccMail, a tiny startup in the LAN-based email. It was a company the VCs wanted to unload and the founder, Hubert Lipinsky, did not want to sell. So, they had told Hubert that if he could find a CEO to re-start the company, they would agree not to sell. The company had only two thousand dollars left in the bank when I joined, and what the VC had not told me is that they had lost interest in the space and didn't want to put any more money into the company and, once I joined, were urging me to sell it.

A year later, the market was getting hot as more LANS were being deployed for file and print sharing, with Microsoft and IBM entering the market with Microsoft Mail and Office Vision. And, despite all the efforts Microsoft made to eliminate us, (I had an interesting discussion at the time with Bill Gates who wanted to acquire us) we succeeded and became the standard in enterprise mail. [The company was sold a few years later to Lotus].

Obstacles

Q: *What are some of the biggest obstacles or challenges you had to overcome to be as successful as you are today?*

A: It's always the internal challenges. We humans are all built with many flaws we have to try to eliminate to become successful. Sometimes flaws may help us for a while—ego, for example—but then they ultimately limit us. The challenge is to find the balance between being driven and keeping the right perspective in mind.

Changing Times

Q: *What do you find most challenging nowadays?*

A: To me these are fascinating days, I enjoy them. Everything is about to change. What I don't really like are the establishments—it's when people are really established, as in their religion, their habits or in their company—that we stop being productive and contribute to progress. We then spend most of our energies protecting what we have instead of thinking of how we could better enjoy, and grow to better enjoy, what we have, and grow a better future for us all.

Q: *Do you think that the American businesses in the Silicon Valley appreciate understanding other persons' cultures in doing business abroad?*

A: If you put things in perspective, for example, if I go back in time and look at France 20 years ago, they believed that their culture was far superior to others'. Today, 20 years later, they still do.

When you look at the "American way of doing business" people 20 years ago, they thought the American way of doing business was the best. Today they are significantly more open, understanding that things are more complex. They have adjusted and are continuing to adjust. The strength of the American system, as it continues to absorb immigrants, is adaptability.

One could say that the European lifestyle is more evolved compared to the American one, but when you spend all your energy protecting what you have, you cannot evolve.

Advice to Foreign-Born Professionals

Q: *What advice would you give French or Chinese or Indians who are either living or coming here?*

A: To the Chinese people I would give different advice. The Chinese people have a unique opportunity coming here to learn the American way of doing business; then they could go back to their country where they have a huge opportunity in front of them.

I was speaking with a group of students in Singapore and that is exactly what I told them. "If you come to America, think that you will have a huge opportunity when you go back. I would say the same thing now to the Indian people." Ten years ago I would have told them, "You come to America and you stay." Today more than 50 percent of start-ups in the Silicon Valley are created by Indians and Chinese and we see more and more of them retuning to their country after their success or failure here.

To the French people I would say, "If you come to America, only go back if you want to be in the leisure industry as I do not see many other opportunities." France will become a country of tourist destinations. French society is not capable at the moment of investing in its future, so how are they going to compete against the globalization of the world? Conversely, France will remain a very unique place where you can come and enjoy yourself, have a vacation.

Guy Gecht, Chairman and CEO, EFI

Guy Gecht
Chairman and CEO, EFI
Country of Origin: Israel
Group: The CEOs

> *"Don't worry about being a foreigner; in general the U.S. is very, very open to foreigners. Learn from this multicultural mix."*

As a student, Guy Gecht played in major bridge tournaments and by the time he was 26, he had played with the Israeli national team. When he came to the U.S., he finally quit. Today he is a high-tech CEO of EFI, quite a switch.

Q: *What are you doing professionally today?*

A: I am the CEO and Chairman of EFI.

Childhood

Q: *How did your childhood experiences and your family influence you to come to where you are today?*

A: I was born in 1965 in Israel. When you grow up in Israel, you grow up on stories of individual leaders in the Army and people leading at the front of the lines. During the 1973 war, my father and my uncles went into the army to fight. It was the worst situation ever; it was exactly the opposite of 1967. We got attacked by surprise by two very, very strong armies. It was a very serious situation. So you grow up on all those war stories and it's a great thing to know you can control forces, you can be in the front, you can think out of the box to win, and you can do things that really matter. Of course this influences your thinking.

Technology Toys

The other thing that influenced me was my interest in software, computers and technology at a young age. I bought the first computer that came out, which was a little Atari, and I played games. My father kept telling me, "You have to understand business, you have to understand economics. You are so focused on technology; it's not good because the geniuses in technology don't make money." It really bothered me. I didn't want to talk about business; I didn't care about that stuff. I had to force myself to think about that.

More Formal Education

Q: *Where did you go to the University?*

A: I finished high school at 17 and then I went to Ben Gurion University in my home town of Be'er Sheva. Soon after I started, the army contacted me and offered to help me finish my engineering degree, if I would then serve in the army.

So after I graduated, I went to officer training school, which by the way, I hated at the time but now I appreciate a lot of the things I learned in that period of my life.

Career Paths

Q: *What did you do after leaving the Army?*

A: I decided to join Apple Europe, which had a goal of competing against the PC in the corporate market. They hired me as the CTO based in Tel Aviv. The problem with that position was that everything I tried to do, the decisions always came from the U.S. I realized that if I wanted to be part of the decision making process, I had to come here to the United States.

So my wife and I made a decision to sell everything we had. We took four suitcases and headed to the U.S. (two of which were stolen as soon as we got here, which made for lighter traveling!). We knew nobody and our idea was to do a coast-to-coast trip and then decide which city we liked the most and find a job there.

We toured the country and the last place we visited was here in the Silicon Valley. I found someone that I knew from Israel who felt strongly I should stay in Silicon Valley; he set me up with an interview. It was the only interview I did in the U.S. and I was offered the job at the end of the interview. The offer wasn't that great, but I needed to get going. It was a balance of long term goals and short term goals.

Start-Ups

A couple of years later, I left to start another company with several other people. We built a great product, which sold really well in the first year, but then there were disagreements about how much we wanted to scale it. So when I got a call from a recruiter about a job at EFI, I thought it was time to work in a bigger company. I heard a lot of great things about EFI, so I joined as a Director of Engineering. Again, I was thinking short term/long term and had the confidence that I could succeed if given the chance. I worked hard and became CEO in 2000.

Obstacles

Q: *What were the biggest obstacles you had to overcome?*

A: I think the biggest obstacle to overcome was the tendency to think you are always right. When you talk to people, you tend to argue to convince them you are right. As you become more senior, the key to being successful is actually to pick up what's the right decision, not to be right. It's actually okay if you're wrong a lot with your original opinion, but end up making the right decision. I had to learn to listen to people and I had to admit mistakes.

Successful Strategies

Q: *What does success mean for you?*

A: You know, success means managing to start something, grow it successfully, and make a difference for people. We are very, very fortunate in our industry to be able to touch so many people's lives. One of the best parts of my job is to see all those companies—small, medium and large—use our products, make money out of them and come back to EFI because they like what we do. We have quality, we have innovation, we have people who trust us, and we take care of our customers so they come back to us. That, in my opinion, is success.

Q: *And what does it mean to you personally?*

A: For me personally, just to feel that I am improving year over year is important. I'm a competitive person. But being competitive is not about money. It's about having a challenge and winning. It's like sports.

Success outside Silicon Valley

Q: *Could you have been as successful outside of the Silicon Valley?*

A: I don't know. It's tough to say. I think there are a lot of things that are similar as far as leadership in business, regardless of where you conduct that business. The great thing about Silicon Valley is that it supports new ideas regardless of your background and helps people from all over to succeed.

Leadership Qualities

Q: *What are the three most important things to do to be a good leader?*

A: First, I think it's very important to understand what is driving the success of your business. Many leaders are just going through the motions of decision after decision. They don't truly understand what is driving their success.

The second quality, which can't be separated from the first, is the ability to articulate your vision. I think every successful leader is someone who can simplify things for people. So I think understanding and articulating are very, very important.

The third is the ability to engage with both your external customers and your internal customers, the employees. You can't be in an ivory tower and send memos: "We have to work harder!" It doesn't really work like that.

Advice

Q: *What advice would you give people coming here to work?*

A: On one hand, I see people who come here to work in the U.S. and they think they can behave as if they were in Israel. That is a big disadvantage. I'll give you just a funny anecdotal example: I came here... and, understand that in Israel, we negotiate everything. Here I went to rent an apartment and it was $1300 a month. So I said, "How about $1100?" They looked at me and said, "What? We don't negotiate here in this country." I said, "What do you mean? They do, too." But only in selective areas like buying a house or a car. So I said, "How about $1200, and give me an extra mirror for free?"

Don't worry about being a foreigner, definitely on the West Coast, but in general, the U.S. is very, very open to foreigners. There's no bias. People are very friendly. What I advise is, "Do your homework." The people here are very smart. There is a reason why the U.S. is such a strong market leader. Learn from this multicultural mix of businesses.

Dan Maydan, CEO Emeritus, Applied Materials

Dan Maydan
CEO Emeritus, Applied Materials
Country of Origin: Israel
Group: The CEOs

> *"Silicon Valley is a very unique place where anyone can succeed depending on his talent and not on his place of origin or the color of his skin. People don't care that they can't even pronounce your name properly as long as you demonstrate capabilities and have respect for others."*

Dan Maydan freely gave me interview time over several visits at his beautiful home in the Los Altos Hills. Though he only gave some information on his philanthropies, from what I heard, he gives away more of his money and his time than he let on in his interview.

Q: *What are you doing professionally today?*

A: After 25 years at Applied Materials, I have retired from the presidency and a year ago I also retired from the Board of Directors. I am a board member of a number of companies—public as well as start-up—helping and strategizing their operations. Also, I am involved with boards of non-profit organizations, such as the Palo Alto Medical Foundation, as well as some universities such as the Technion.

Childhood Influences

Q: *How did your childhood experiences or your family influence you to follow the path you took?*

A: I grew up in Israel, which continuously struggled to survive; my parents escaped Russia in the early 1920s and came to Palestine as Zionists, working hard to build Israel to what it is today. Struggling to survive, one of the priorities was the proper education of the children.

University and Marriage

I graduated from the Technion in 1957, at the age of 21 and joined the Israel Atomic Energy Commission. One year later, I became in charge of the Electronics Group of the newly built research reactor. During my employment, in 1959, I met my wife. Both of us worked for the Atomic Energy Commission and at the same time, I completed my Master's Degree at the Technion while my wife completed a Ph.D. Degree. We got married in 1960 and in 1962, our daughter was born. A few months later, in August 1962, we all left for Edinburgh where I studied for a Ph.D. in nuclear physics.

Q: *Why did you choose Edinburgh?*

A: We decided for various reasons to study in Great Britain, at Edinburgh University. I was offered a fellowship while my wife got a teaching job. We stayed there for three years and after completing my Ph.D., we all came back to Israel where I worked at the Ministry of Defense in Haifa.

Move to the U.S. and Applied Materials

In 1965, a few months after we returned to Israel, our son was born. In 1967, the family moved to the U.S. where I worked for Bell Telephone

Labs in New Jersey and my wife taught at Rutgers University. In 1969, our third child was born.

I worked for Bell Labs for 13 years. During my last few years at Bell Labs, I decided to get involved more in business aspects rather than just in R&D. I wanted to be able to communicate and deliver high-tech products to customers. I formed a group with two of my colleagues, David Wang and Sass Somekh, and we searched for funds to start a new company. During that process, we came across a small company, Applied Materials. After many months of negotiations, my partners and I signed an agreement to join Applied in order to develop a Plasma Etch business.

Joining forces with some of the existing management team of Applied Materials, we created and built the company to become the leader of the semiconductor process equipment industry. In 25 years, the company grew from about $30 million annual revenue into a global $10 billion company.

Q: *How did you keep on putting in the amount of work that must have been necessary to make the company so successful?*

A: The most important factor of my success was my wife. We had a unique marriage; she was not just a very talented scientist, but the most wonderful and wise person. We had such harmony in our lives that I was able to concentrate and focus on my job.

Q: *Did you talk to her about your work?*

A: The discussions around the table were about children, politics and science. My wife used to say, “It is amazing that both of us have a similar education and still, I love science because of its beauty, whereas my husband tells me that the only important part of science for him is its application to improve life.”

Obstacles?

Q: *What were some of the biggest obstacles you had to overcome if you look at your career?*

A: I cannot recall major obstacles. I always defined my goals very clearly and made sure that I could meet my objectives.

Being a Foreigner in Silicon Valley

Q: *Did your being a foreigner originally help you working in the U.S.?*

A: I don't think it helped me; except as an immigrant, you want to prove yourself and work very hard to accomplish what you have set out to do. I participated in building Applied Materials as a company "built to last" and an ideal family life made it all possible.

Silicon Valley is a very unique place where anyone can succeed depending on his talent and not on his place of origin or the color of his skin. People don't care that they can't even pronounce your name properly as long as you demonstrate capabilities and have respect for others.

Advice

Q: *What advice would you give to Israelis who live here or are coming to work?*

A: It all depends on the individual aspirations, but I think that one needs to maintain one's ethics, to be hard-working and contribute to society by doing what one knows and can do best. There's nothing more important than that—to really aspire to success and compete as hard as one can, but in a very positive way.

Definition of Success

Q: *What does it mean to you to be successful?*

A: That changes with age. At a young age, success is if you meet your goals. You set goals for yourself, and if you meet them, or go beyond them, you are successful. At a later age, that is not sufficient; you want to leave your mark on society by giving back and improving life around you.

Dalia Maydan

Dan and Dalia Maydan

My first priority is to ensure the success of the Dalia Maydan Advanced Materials Science Institute at the Technion, built in memory of my late wife, Dalia, which I visit on a yearly basis, and try to help ensure its success.

Seeing the building filled with young people studying for the future, some of whom will become the leaders in the high-tech world of tomorrow, gives me deep satisfaction.

Chapter

8 Overseas Entrepreneur

Not everyone interviewed in this book has his/her business directly in Silicon Valley; some of the foreign executives operate out of their own country, but do business in the U.S. and on a global scale.

Khaled Olayan is such a unique businessman. When I had the opportunity to interview him (by telephone), I knew I had to include him in the book. His Middle Eastern, Saudi background is one that is not often seen from a personal view. He and his company are so exceptional that I wanted the readers to be able to hear his story.

Khaled Olayan, Chairman, The Olayan Group

Khaled Olayan
Chairman, The Olayan Group
Country of Origin: Saudi Arabia
Group: The Overseas Entrepreneur

> *"Probably one of the greatest ingredients for personal happiness is to not only focus on what one can get through one's career, but what one can give. Young people should ask themselves how they can make a meaningful contribution to their organizations and to society at large."*

Khaled S. Olayan is truly an extraordinary leader. Even though he is the chairman of a hugely successful enterprise, his attitude is surprisingly humble. What is especially visible from the interview below—via phone—is his dedication to education, to excellence, and to the support of the people working for him, regardless of gender, nationality or family affiliation.

Khaled Olayan understands the importance of maintaining a global view of the world to keep his Group and its diverse operations on an even keel and to be truly competitive. At the same time, he understands the importance of focusing also on his home country, where the Olayan enterprise was founded 60 years ago, in 1947.

He remains true to the philosophy of his late father, who believed that a good education is one of the most important influences in a young person's life.

Childhood Influences

Q: *How did your childhood influence you where you are today in your career?*

A: My childhood was greatly influenced by a progression from a traditional oasis village in Saudi Arabia to a larger commercial town to cosmopolitan Beirut and multicultural Lebanon. My world view kept expanding.

The people who influenced me the most as a child were my father and his older brother, my uncle. I spent quite some time with them and saw the way they were working, the way they were running things. They built their businesses the old-fashioned way, with total dedication and commitment, and thus derived great personal satisfaction from the work.

My father, in particular, instilled in me that one should always strive to do one's best, to do what one's conscience dictates, to respect and earn others' respect, and to do something for society and the community. My father put a lot of emphasis on hard work and thrift. One should be modest and humble, never flashy or extravagant.

Role of Education

Q: *What education did you get to prepare you for what you are doing now as Chairman of The Olayan Group?*

A: First of all I went to high school in Lebanon when I was a teenager. That gave me a good platform to start school in the U.S.

I went to Menlo College in Atherton, California, and after that I went to American University in Washington, DC to get my MBA, after which I went back home.

Definition of Success

Q: *What does your success mean to you?*

A: I learned a lot from my late father who was the founder and the chairman of our company. He was a self-established entrepreneur, and he was somewhat of a walking university himself, because he had an absolutely exceptional memory and just retained everything about his business, the companies with whom he dealt and in which he invested, facts and figures, numbers and, most especially, people. I learned a lot from him. One main thing I learned is that success is really simply a matter of always doing better tomorrow what you do today.

Business Differences—Arab Culture

Q: *What do you differently when you do business in Saudi Arabia, than you would do when you are dealing with Americans?*

A: We [the Arab culture] are different, whether rightly or wrongly, nevertheless, there is a lot of social etiquette, which really can often confuse people.

It's not like doing business with the Americans where you go in, state your point, and make a decision—okay, finished, we agree or we don't agree and then goodbye. In our culture you have social courtesies, courtesies that have to be practiced. There is a certain time you have to take with your counterpart. I suppose this is an important element in how we carry out our due diligence. We think it is important to know our counterpart informally, on a personal level to some extent, so that a degree of familiarity and comfort with one another is established before considering any commitments. Investing time in the process of building personal trust and confidence is crucial in our culture, I would say. In addition, there are certain cultural rituals you have to be aware of.

Q: *Can you name me one or two of them?*

I guess the best example in Saudi culture is the ritual of drinking Arab "coffee," which is brewed from cardamom and served with local dates, which are a matter of great pride in Saudi Arabia. There are protocols in the coffee ritual. For example, it is considered polite to accept three tiny cups and then no more. We also have rather precise kissing rituals within our culture between men, but we don't generally extend this practice to foreigners unless they know us very, very well. Obviously, the potential for misunderstanding in this area can be great. On formal occasions, we often burn incense as a fragrance, a sign of great hospitality and respect for one's guests. These are just a few examples.

I would also say that in general, business relationships in our culture tend to last a much longer time in the Middle East and in Saudi Arabia, in particular, than in the West, assuming the business partners are compatible. There is flavor to the relationship, emotional involvement. The families get to know each other among partners because the kids go to the same schools. There are more ties that develop in the relationship, besides the business. So this is where our culture is different.

Objective Governance

Q: *Why did you choose a non-relative to be the President and CEO of The Olayan Group?*

A: I would say that we chose Aziz Syriani, who is of Lebanese origin, not specifically because he is non-family. Rather, we chose the best possible person for the job. Aziz is a Harvard-trained international lawyer who is just brilliant. He has been a fellow employee of the Group for 30 years and before that was outside counsel. I suppose that as a non-family member, he brings a certain objectivity to our corporate table, which we highly value. But as a Group, we prize professionalism, integrity, commitment and trust above the issue of family or non-family. The absolutely essential thing is to employ good people who work hard for the best interests of our common enterprise.

Q: *Isn't your Group the exception? Is that something that is coming up in other parts of Saudi Arabia as well?*

A: No, I think that is how we do it ourselves. The others in Saudi Arabia, from my knowledge and from being close to some of my friends who run similar groups, they are all family-run and their executives report to them. The key positions are in the family members' hands, but we don't necessarily follow that line ourselves. Although my sisters are in the family, they rose to CEO based on merit, and their companies under them are some of the most successful in the group. They earned their spot.

Multicultural Leadership

Q: *Tell me please what are the greatest challenges for multicultural leaders today where you can't just do U.S. business or Saudi business?*

A: You know, there are several challenges. I guess it goes without saying that English language competence is absolutely essential. Also, our world has shrunk measurably in this new age of globalization, so a global perspective is absolutely key. Issues like global warming, terrorism, infectious disease and energy supply and demand are all cross-border issues that affect everyone. At the same time, the fluidity of international capital means that all investors, everywhere today, are in some sense global. On the trade and investment fronts, the WTO is really foreshadowing the world, bringing an agreed-upon set of international norms to all corners of the earth and all nations, regardless of their particular historic past or current form of governance. These norms or standards have to do with openness and market access, transparency, accountability and the rule of law. As the international playing field becomes level like never before, competition will increase. This is positive for business and consumers alike. But to be competitive, we all have to work harder on quality and qualifications, whether in business or in education and training. Both the private and public sectors must be fully engaged.

So this, to me, is a major, major challenge we are going to face here in Saudi Arabia. We have to know where our limits are, and we have to look towards a more diversified future beyond just energy and oil resources. This process has begun in Saudi Arabia, with many new projects and initiatives in all sectors under way or planned.

Q: *Don't you in Saudi Arabia also have a greater percentage of young people under the age of 25?*

A: Oh, yes. As a matter of fact you have touched on a very sensitive and important point; more than 50 percent of our population is under the age of 21.

We have a lot of the young generation that needs to be well educated, trained, properly placed in the right positions, attended to and groomed to be competent professionals and good leaders.

Leader Qualifications

Q: *Please tell me what three things are important to be an effective leader.*

A: One thing I believe, Ms. Blendstrup, is that leadership is not inherited. You have to grow into it. While certain attributes of good leaders may be innate—extroversion or social intelligence, for example—effective business leaders, at least, are more often made through experience than simply being born into it, in my judgment.

Q: *So, leadership can be acquired?*

A: I think it can be acquired. I think leadership is as much an attitude as anything else. Charisma is probably innate. But effective leadership is not just charisma. Maybe you can win elections with just charisma, a sparkling and magnetic personality, but you cannot win the trust of the people. Charisma doesn't guarantee integrity or competence or sound judgment, and all these things are crucial in business leadership. So anyone can aspire to be a business leader—to motivate both by example and by encouraging and supporting and rewarding those who work for you. Mutual respect and teamwork are also key. Respect others and they will respect you. All these things reflect a certain attitude about oneself and one's place in the world rather than any innate ability. I think this is especially true in our culture, which places a very great premium on modesty in all things and on governing and managing through consensus rather than individual willfulness. To be a successful leader, your people have to be successful with you. This is the only way to lead to success—and you cannot do it alone.

Advice

Q: *What advice would you give to Saudis who are living in Saudi Arabia and who want to come here to Silicon Valley, for instance, to work?*

A: Whether in Saudi Arabia or outside, it is important to know where you want to go and what you want to achieve and then work very hard to get there. Becoming really competent in English is essential in today's world and, of course, you have to achieve the greatest possible mastery of your chosen field. Being an objective and good critical thinker is certainly important. So is being a life-long learner. You can never know enough. You can never stop learning. Ambition and drive are key, too, but so is humility.

But probably one of the greatest ingredients for personal happiness is to not only focus on what one can get through one's career, but what one can give. Young people should ask themselves how they can make a meaningful contribution to their organizations and to society at large. How can I achieve good in the world? Surely, that is one of the best motivators of all.

Chapter

9 Philanthropic Entrepreneurs

Some entrepreneurs stand out because of their focus on giving back. Listen to the stories of the philanthropists:

- Kamran Elahian, Chairman, Co-Founder, Global Catalyst Partners
- Charly Kleissner, Co-Founder, KL Felicitas Foundation

Kamran Elahian, Chairman and Co-Founder, Global Catalyst Partners

Kamran Elahian
Chairman and Co-Founder, Global Catalyst Partners
Country of Origin: Iran
Group: Philanthropic Entrepreneur

> *"Many times as a leader, you find that you were wrong, that the younger person had a better way of doing something. Through that process you also learn and don't become a fossil."*

Kamran made time in his busy schedule to stop by my house for our interview. His interview is a series of life's events, told in funny stories. More stories will be available on my web site.

Current Profession

Q: *Please tell me what you are doing professionally today.*

A: I'm a venture capital investor in the high-tech industry. The name of our firm is Global Catalyst Partners. We invest in the leading edge technology companies in the United States, China, India, Japan and Israel.

Childhood Influences

Q: *How did your childhood lead you to where you are today?*

A: I grew up in Iran until the age of 18. As a child I always had a vision for big things. I felt I had to do something to change the world, something that matters. I remember at times looking at some of my relatives and they seemed so preoccupied only with their own lives. That always surprised me.

Q: *Did your parents influence you and open your eyes to that, or was that just something that came to you naturally?*

A: My mom was highly educated; she spoke four languages. She had always instilled in me that I should be culturally aware. She definitely had an influence. My father was very street smart, he had to leave his village at the age of 12. He became a self-made man, a very successful entrepreneur who learned everything on the job. He felt that, because he didn't have much of a chance to get an education himself, he wanted to push us to have a good education. I remember taking many extra courses in English as a Second Language, because he always wanted me to excel in English.

Another influence from my background is that my parents and grandparents lived through many ups and downs in life. My grandfather was killed by Stalin; his family was thrown out of Russia and had to go back to Iran. From my mother's side, I knew how refugees feel about things. And because of the Iranian Revolution, my family lost its whole fortune.

Religious Influences

Q: *Did they leave Iran or did they stay there?*

A: They were actually in the U.S. when the Revolution happened, they were a religious minority, and they were *Baha'is*.

Q: *I heard that there are only two million Baha'is in the world, is that true?*

A: I don't know the exact number. This religion started in Iran and spread globally. I'm not a Baha'i, but I know because I was raised as one. It's a very modern religion, only a couple of hundred years old. The Prophet had a global vision: all human beings are the same, their rights should be preserved.

One of the things that the Western World has not understood is that Iran has been the birthplace of a number of prophets with a global outlook such as Zoroaster, Rumi and Baha'ullah.

Q: *Did your parents continue to follow their beliefs?*

A: Absolutely. They still do. To be a Baha'i you have to believe in Muhammad, in Jesus, in Moses; you have to believe in Zoroaster, in all the previous Prophets.

Baha'i is quite unique as a religion in that you have to search for truth two times in your life—once at 16, once at 21. If you declare the belief both times, it is solid and you can declare yourself a Baha'i. I did it at the age of 16, but when I was 21, I changed my mind and did not declare.

Q: *Please give me a quick overview of how you got to where you are today?*

A: I was doing pretty well in high school in Iran and until the age of 16. I was always number one or number two in my class. But, when I started going through puberty, I became quite a rebel. I got involved in politics, fought for freedom, and had many encounters with SAVAK (the secret police).

Under the Shah we had a dictatorship. It was pretty bad, but unfortunately, it was replaced by an even worse one.

Q: *So your parents were happy when you went to the United States?*

A: Yes. They were happy that I left Iran and came to the U.S. The U.S. was definitely a different kind of country: the land of freedom and opportunity.

The Trek to Silicon Valley

Q: *Tell me how you finally got to Silicon Valley?*

A: I got two Bachelor's Degrees from the University of Utah at the age of 20, and finished my Master's in Computer Graphics by the age of 22. A year later, I started looking for a job in California and landed at Hewlett-Packard; I worked in their corporate engineering lab in Palo Alto.

Using computer graphics, I developed software to help mask designers with the design of integrated circuit chips. I was quite curious about all these rectangles that go on top of each other and create electrical elements called "transistors."

At that time a friend of mine, Jim Clark, was a professor at Stanford and he introduced me to two professors, John Newkirk and Rob Matthews, who were teaching a class on new methodology for IC design. They said that any systems or software engineer can learn to do chip design.

I talked to my bosses at HP and they agreed to pay my tuition to Stanford to take courses in chip design. I designed a chip, it was fabricated and came back but it didn't work. I went back to the professors and said, "You said any system or software engineer could do this. How come my chip is not working?" They answered, "Well, any *good* system or software engineer can do that, you are not a very good engineer." So that was the end of my distinguished technical career!

Q: *That must not have been easy.*

A: It was fascinating because, as an entrepreneur, when you are faced with difficulties, you see opportunities.

I came up with an idea, went to my boss and said, "Why don't we use computer graphics to design an interactive system that is targeted towards engineers rather than IC mask designers? Give me another half a million dollar budget, a few more engineers, and then I'll go and build this system."

At that time I was 27. My boss said to me, "Kamran, you are the most ambitious person I've ever met. Every six months, you want more money, more people to work with—you are just a kid. It took me five years to become a manager, but you are already there, you have done all these different things." I replied, "Well, in that case, I will leave." He said, "Fine, I'm tired of this."

Then his boss came and tried to convince me to stay, but he didn't succeed. Then the boss' boss came and talked to me, also trying to convince me to stay. He took me to lunch to a Chinese restaurant and he told me about start-ups and how 50 percent of them fail within the first year, 90 percent within five years. The waiter brought us fortune cookies. I opened mine.

Q: *What did your fortune cookie say?*

A: I read it and started laughing and he asked, "What is it?" I said, "No, I can't show it to you, it's too embarrassing." But he insisted, so I showed it to him, and the fortune cookie said, "Do not listen to him, you will be successful." So that's what determined my life—a fortune cookie!

Q: *That's a wonderful story.*

A: This was in 1981; I decided to leave and took a few engineers with me. Very few VCs existed at that time and finding them was very difficult, but we finally got money and it was quite a bit. We had lots of ups and downs, but it helped to create a whole new market. We created a high-tech company called CAE-Systems (Computer Aided Engineering).

It was only three years later, I wasn't even 30 years old, when HP first expressed an interest in acquiring the company. But then Tektronix came in with an offer of $75 million, to which we couldn't say no.

Q: *Which at that time was quite unheard of.*

A: It was unbelievable. The second company I was involved with was called Cirrus Logic. Suhas [Patil, see his interview in Start-Up Wizards], the original founder, was a former professor at the University of Utah.

Although I had never taken courses from him, I always liked him, not only because he was teaching hardware and chip design but because he was quite far ahead of his time. I also liked him because, even though I was not a scholar and not even in his department, he was always kind hearted; he would sit down and talk with me.

When he started Cirrus, he had some difficulties. So he packed his bags, came here to Silicon Valley and we worked together for the next five years. First I thought it might become another software company. But we decided it should be a chip company. Although, in fact, it was too advanced and unusual in the way it was designing chips.

Third Start-Up

After Cirrus Logic's IPO, I decided to leave and start another company, my third one. At the time, I thought, "Why not put a team together that could revolutionize the PC business?"

I started a company called Momenta. By this time the VCs had all become great believers and they quickly gave me $40 million. We spent it all. I had become quite aggressive, I thought I couldn't make mistakes—we were developing a revolutionary computer that would use a pen and paper metaphor instead of a keyboard. When we introduced it, we were on the cover of 20 magazines as "The Future of Computing." I was so sure we would succeed that I promised $100 million of revenues for the first year.

Unfortunately, the sales were less than $3 million and I got fired on April 1st, 1992. I'll never forget that day. I went to my office and saw there was a board meeting. I said, "I'm the Chairman and CEO, I didn't call a board meeting." They replied, "Not anymore." I thought it was an April Fool's joke; however, they were darn serious.

Life's Changes

Anyway, this probably had the biggest impact on my life, because I was 38 years old when this happened. I thought this would be "the" time to get to know myself better, because the big four-oh was coming.

I reflected, *"What am I going to do with my life?"* The more I studied history, the more I noticed that people had two choices: they could either trade or get what they wanted by force. There had to be a way for people to know each other better, to work with and trade with each other peacefully and beneficially to all.

The Three Pillars—a Personal Philosophy

This thought process created the three pillars of my beliefs.

The First Pillar

The first pillar was that instead of just creating a company to revolutionize the market and or develop a cool product, why not develop technologies that would bring the world closer together? It would get people to interact and to learn more about each other. These types of technologies include communications and mobility.

The Second Pillar

The second pillar was to create companies that are global from day one and that become the vehicle that allows people to interact.

If you look at Cirrus, not only did we start Cirrus Logic in the U.S., but also in Japan, Taiwan and Germany. This gave me an understanding of doing business globally. A company should look at the whole world to do business with.

The Third Pillar

And then the third pillar was the consideration, *"What do you need your money for?"* You buy a house and a couple of nice cars and those should satisfy your needs in life. So why not give the money away on a global basis and create a path for peace, build bridges?

Why not create global foundations and have activities in different countries? This can be done through education, providing rights for women—especially empowering women—using microcredit cooperatives and computers to educate them and their children. Then the whole world becomes a lot better.

So I put this into action. Each one of these three pillars drove all my decisions from that point on.

NeoMagic

The next company I created, NeoMagic, developed chips and enabled the creation of a new generation of laptop computers (e.g., Sony VAIO and IBM ThinkPad).

It actually broke the record of Cirrus Logic, and Cirrus itself had broken the record of all semiconductor companies in its time. Cirrus went from zero to a billion dollars in less than ten years. Our third year revenue at NeoMagic was $240 million. We were just going through the roof, the Sony VAIO and the IBM ThinkPad were created because we enabled them to use our technology.

My biggest success actually came later.

My sixth company was Centillium Communications. We developed ADSL [Asymmetric Digital Subscriber Line] chips for high speed communication.

Our first year revenue was $56 million, our second year $160 million. We went public in the summer of 2000 (after the burst of the Bubble). Our market cap on the day of the IPO was $700 million, and within a year, our market cap was over $4 billion.

Creating Global Companies

Q: *Are you having fun?*

A: Oh, yes, I am! Talk about really connecting the whole world together! All of my companies give people the technology to enable mobility—to connect and exchange ideas. If people interact with each other, they lose their xenophobia and start to form relationships.

In terms of creating global companies, in 1999, I co-founded Global Catalyst Partners. We have a $300 million fund that invests in early stage companies in the U.S., China, India, Japan and Israel. We have a team with a diverse background; we come from China, Japan, India, Iran and the U.S., a mini-United Nations in action.

Implementing the third pillar, I founded Schools Online; a global foundation that has worked with schools in 36 countries. Starting in 1996, we donated computers to over 6,400 schools, and connected them to the Internet. We want to reach the kids at a young age so they learn how to use the Internet for virtual global travel and become citizens of the world.

Once these kids grow up, they will not be easily manipulated by a corrupt religious leader, or political leaders who want to start a war. These kids will say, "I have already exchanged so many IMs and emails with kids from other cultures that I know that they are not that bad. They are just like me, why should I fight with them?"

Three Essential Qualities of a Leader

Q: *What would you say are the three greatest things an effective leader has to have today?*

A: First of all, if you understand the mega trends, understand the world from a global perspective, you can lead your organization, your company, your community in ways that take advantage of these trends, rather than going against them.

Second, I think what is also necessary for a leader is integrity. You must have integrity in what you say and in what you do. You need to set a good example and people will follow.

The third thing to have as a leadership style, is to be able to empower people. I think it is really important to let people come up with ideas and have tolerance for their ways, even if you think they are going to fail—let them, give them some room so they can fail a little and learn from it.

Charly Kleissner, Co-Founder, KL Felicitas Foundation

Karl "Charly" Kleissner
Co-Founder, KL Felicitas Foundation
Country of Origin: Austria
Group: Philanthropic Entrepreneur

> *"Success to me means living a purposeful life where I leverage my talents to provide a meaningful and impacting contribution towards a more sustainable planet from an economic, environmental, social and spiritual perspective."*

Charly is a breath of fresh air, with his enthusiasm for his ventures and his optimism that he is contributing to making the world a better place. We sat down together at my house when he was on a break in his tight travel schedule.

Q: *What are you doing professionally today?*

A: I call myself a "philanthropic entrepreneur." We know what entrepreneurism is about. It's about being creative and innovative. It is driving systemic change, taking risks, not taking no for an answer and managing change on an ongoing basis. We question if the older model of just giving out grants is the best model for achieving systemic change.

Grants

Q: *What kind of grants to do you give and to whom?*

A: Our foundation is focused on two main programs: supporting social entrepreneurs worldwide (helping them develop and grow economically sustainable, scalable enterprises with high measurable social impact) and supporting rural communities globally.

Q: *Can you give me an example of whom you give grants to?*

A: A great example of a successful grant relationship is Lalith Seneviratne in Sri Lanka whom we've been working with for the last two years. When we were visiting Lalith and his family about two and a half years ago to work on LED lighting systems for rural communities in Sri Lanka, he was implementing community-based electrification systems based on solar electricity and biomass. We worked with him to scale his nascent electrification effort up from two villages to 20 villages.

Investment Criteria

When we evaluate social entrepreneurs, we use three criteria. The first one is whether they want to scale their social enterprise. The second investment criterion is: they have to have an understanding and a desire for what it would take to get to economic sustainability. The third one is that we really demand accountability of social and environmental metrics.

Early Childhood Influences

Q: *How did your childhood and your family influence you to get where you are now?*

A: I was brought up in Innsbruck, Austria, and went to high school there. I think the biggest credit has to go to my father, as he contributed the most to my deep desire of leaving Innsbruck and exploring the world. As a matter of fact, when I was 16, I applied for a scholarship and ended up in Hawaii, so I spent one year in 1974–1975 in Hawaii and I had a wonderful time. I met my wife Lisa there—I was 17 at the time.

University Studies

Then I went back to Innsbruck and wanted to study something that was not available there, as I had outgrown my home town. Computer Science was just being offered for the first time in 1974, and so I decided to go to the Vienna University of Technology to study Computer Science in 1975. In that year, I learned how to program with punch cards. In 1976, the Apple II became a hit.

Austrian Society and Women

My wife, Lisa, joined me in Austria in 1982 and we got married in 1983. I was in the middle of my Ph.D. program, which I finished in 1985. We had our son Alex in 1984 and then in 1985, Lisa, as a professional architect, wanted to work in Austria.

But it turned out that the Austrian society at that time was pretty conservative vis-à-vis non-Austrian, professional women and so the opportunities were not really there. She suggested we go to the United States. Since I am much more of a practical, hands-on activist than a theoretician, we decided that I should try to get a job in Silicon Valley because that's where the action was.

Getting to Silicon Valley

When I first visited in 1985, I realized I had no connections. Therefore I started going to conferences and giving speeches about my thesis, which was about distributed systems database systems and transaction systems. I started building up my network and I handed out my resume, which of course had no real practical jobs on it—just teaching and researching. It was very tough and it took me nine months to get to the job offer stage and then I finally received three job offers at the same time. I chose Hewlett-Packard and became the technical leader of the distributed database system team.

In 1986, Hewlett-Packard relocated us over from Vienna, just two months after our daughter Andrea was born. They offered us full reimbursement of all moving costs and we only had one possession that barely filled up one third of the container [laughter]. And that was our piano.

Understanding Silicon Valley

I stayed with Hewlett-Packard for three years and although my performance was consistently rated exceptional, my salary kept on getting less and less in comparison to my peer group, so after three years, I was ready to move on!

I made a move to Digital Equipment Corporation and during the five years there, I started understanding how Silicon Valley really works and that it's all about leverage and networking. I had set my sights on becoming a VP of Engineering at an A company and so I started to figure out what I needed to do to get there. I joined Digital Equipment Corporation to get second level management experience and I managed a section or multiple teams of managers. I made management mistakes but I learned a lot.

Future Plans—Apple

Then, I remember going on a winter camping trip with Lisa, and reflecting and planning our future, and we decided that I was done with the big corporations. It became clear that I was ready to do the start-up game, get the equity, and ultimately become the VP of Engineering of a great start-up.

I had always been intrigued by what Steve Jobs had done early on at Apple, but Apple was already big and so I said to myself, "I want to go work for Steve at NeXT." I did my research and connected to their CTO and found out that they needed management talent. I remember my interview with Steve at Il Fornaio in Palo Alto for breakfast. He had two huge orange juices and some muesli and I had eggs. This interview sealed the deal, and I became Director of Engineering for Steve in 1993.

I was not a VP yet, but I was at the director level, which is one level below, and I really, really learned a tremendous amount about productivity and high-energy teams, motivations, etc. Steve is both an asset and a liability and he challenged everyone on his team to come up with products and ideas and that's when I learned about how few greatly qualified and dedicated people it takes to make a revolution and an impact.

I worked there for three years and we had sort of a triumvirate of management. One VP left and Steve tried to figure out how to structure his most senior team. I didn't see a chance of making it to the next level at that time. I also understood that I would not yet get a chance to be the top engineering executive at an A-level company.

Moving to DataMind

Therefore I looked around for a solid B-level company to go to next, and found DataMind, which was a good opportunity—a solid company poised for growth even though it was a challenging turnaround situation. It was tough to leave Jobs because he wanted to keep me. We had a long conversation at his house, but in the end, he respected my decision, which I still value because he understood that at this stage in my career, I wanted to take the next step and he couldn't offer that to me. Therefore, he wished me well and I created a solid engineering team at DataMind.

The next opportunity came along, which was the A-level opportunity I was always looking for and that was Ariba. I became their engineering leader and Senior VP of Product Development.

Spiritual and Philanthropic Journey

Q: *How did you get into foundation work?*

A: After I left Ariba, I went on a journey that was both spiritual and philanthropic to figure out a more meaningful way of spending the rest of my life. I discovered a book entitled *From Success to Significance* by Lloyd Reeb, and that became my mantra at that time. In 2000, Lisa convinced me that creating a family foundation was a good thing.

Obstacles

Q: *What were the biggest obstacles you had to overcome in life?*

A: Getting the first job in the U.S. was a huge obstacle. I sent my resume to well over 100 places and tried to get interviews, etc. When I didn't get any traction for months, it was very hard not to get discouraged. But having a strong vision and lots of perseverance helped me through that.

Success—A Different Understanding

Q: *What does it mean to you to be successful?*

A: We talked a lot about my success in my early career, about becoming the VP of Engineering of an A company in Silicon Valley, so that was my success criterion for the first half of my life.

Success to me means living a purposeful life where I leverage my talents to provide a meaningful and impacting contribution towards a more sustainable planet from an economic, environmental, social and spiritual perspective.

Role of Silicon Valley

Q: *Could you have done this outside of Silicon Valley? Could you have been as successful?*

A: No, I would not have been able to accomplish what I did outside of Silicon Valley. And I would not be able to do what I do today without having spent 20 years in the vortex of high technology, helping shape the information society as we know it today—participating and creating innovative and creative business and technology solutions for complex issues. This experience gave me the tools and the know-how necessary to tackle my current goals. Silicon Valley is unique in the world. There is no other place on the planet with a similar level of creative, innovative, out-of-the-box type thinking and energy.

Multicultural Leadership

Q: *What do you think are the challenges for multicultural leadership today?*

A: Let me start out with a couple of personal observations. I tend to sometimes demand too strong a professional management behavior from the social entrepreneurs I work with internationally, without sensitivity to the cultural context that I'm in. Especially in our work in rural India and rural Sri Lanka, the level on which we demand results or the urgency that we demand to get something done, doesn't necessarily work in the local context. We need to be more respectful and understanding of the context and listen to what's going on in order to be successful in multicultural environments.

Advice

Q: *What advice would you give to people who want to come here?*

A: I would say, don't worry about your title, about the corner office, about your status. Do a great job when you get here, work with people you like to work with, surround yourself with people who inspire you, make a contribution, and then great things are going to follow.

Chapter 10 The American Hosts

It might seem strange to include a last group of people who did not cross an ocean to get here. These executives are distinguished by the role they played as hosts to the immigrants. They help create the unique ecosystem of Silicon Valley and exhibit a willingness to work with their overseas counterparts who come to work here. Many profited handsomely as a result of this willingness to partner with creative people from across the planet. Their attitude to outsiders contrasts to those displayed in many other parts of the world. You probably won't find a group like this as easily in Japan, France, Germany or the UK—where the homegrown elites "play their cards close to their chest" and are worse off because of it.

One of the unique features of Silicon Valley is openness to innovation from any source. This applies to people's backgrounds as much as to technology. These people tell the stories of the American Hosts:

- John Hennessy, President, Stanford University
- The Honorable George Shultz, former U.S. Secretary of State, Hoover Institute, Stanford University

- Eric Schmidt, CEO, Google, written statement
- Scott McNealy, Co-Founder and Chairman, Sun Microsystems, written statement
- Vinton Cerf, Chief Evangelist, Google
- Steve Westly, Founder and CEO, The Westly Group
- Guy Kawasaki, Managing Director, Garage Technology Ventures
- Nat Goldhaber, Managing Director, Claremont Creek Ventures

John Hennessy, President, Stanford University

John Hennessy
President, Stanford University
Country of Origin: U.S.
Group: The American Hosts

> *"If you're a founder in a company, with that comes a certain mantle of responsibility, which puts you in a position of doing things… that forces you to learn how to navigate in very stormy waters."*

John Hennessy is constantly dashing to his many commitments as President of Stanford University. However, he gave me back his transcribed interview in a matter of days—completely edited!

John Hennessy and MIPS

John Hennessy describes himself as the reluctant entrepreneur, but one for whom the entrepreneurial experience was truly transformative. As the President of Stanford University, he can look back with a critical but enthusiastic eye on founding MIPS Computer Systems, the company that first commercialized RISC architecture. Inspiration for starting a company came from C. Gordon Bell, one of the pioneers of the computer industry.

> "The industry was extremely skeptical. There was interest in the DEC local research lab on the West Coast. By and large the mainstream was ignoring us. Gordon Bell came by and said, "You guys should start a company to build this technology, because if you don't, it's going to sit on the shelf. It's too disruptive to the established players for them to do it."

As an academic, Hennessy hadn't really wanted to start a company, and he planned to return to Stanford.

> "My role as Chief Scientist was always, from the beginning, that I was going to go back to the university after spending about a year full-time on it, then be involved on a part-time, consulting, summer basis."

But that year (which became a year-and-a-half) and Hennessy's subsequent experiences with entrepreneurship had a significant impact on him.

> "It probably was the single most formative year of my life. I learned so much in that year. People who are in engineering disciplines and spend their whole times in academia really don't understand what it's like in companies. They don't understand how people make decisions... You realize the difference between a product and something you have in a laboratory... You learn about leading people and managing teams, you learn a lot about focus. And you learn that there is a great reward when you build a product and people use it."

One of the most fascinating aspects of Hennessy's experience is its impact on his perceptions about technology transfer.

> "More often than not, the right technology transfer path for a new innovation was a start-up rather than an existing market company. It really taught me the difficulty of transforming. The more disruptive the technology is, the higher the probably it has to be transferred by a start-up. You see that time and time again. If we had a discovery that is directly useful for some company's product line, that's fine, then they know how to license it. If you have something that represents a new opportunity for them to establish a whole new product line, that's much harder for them."

At the same time, he has first-hand experience of the entrepreneurial roller-coaster. The experience of founding a technology-based start-up brings responsibilities and learning opportunities. For Hennessy, it was almost a short detour from a professional career that has led from his first faculty position at Stanford in 1977 to the University President's office. But it was a detour that helped him develop skills, and it's not unreasonable to believe that this short, formative experience contributed to taking on more responsibilities—including administrative leadership roles at the University and a seat on the Board of both Cisco and Google.

> "Learning to be a professor is important, but all the other skills that I learned about being an administrator, dean, provost and president, I probably learned more from the time I spent in the start-up and subsequent entrepreneurial activities than I learned anywhere else."

There are few experiences quite like starting a technology-based spin-out of a university research project. Though Hennessy never doubted his place at the University, he knows the value of the environment of the start-up, and the impact on the founders.

> "If you're a founder in a company, with that comes a certain mantle of responsibility, which puts you in a position of doing things... that forces you to learn how to navigate in very stormy waters. Those are things that prepare you very well to do that on a larger scale subsequently. It also prepares you to focus and make decisions. At small companies, you have to decide. That's a skill set that's absolutely crucial, to be able to make decisions on less than perfect information, and it happens all the time... I learned more in that year than I learned in any five years of my life. And it's fun."

The Honorable George Shultz, former U.S. Secretary of State, Hoover Institute, Stanford University

The Honorable George Shultz
Former U.S. Secretary of State, Hoover Institute Fellow in International Affairs, Stanford University
Country of Origin: U.S
Group: The American Hosts

> *"The willingness to let people fail is very important because it gives flexibility to the economy. There are something like 600,000 new enterprises started each year in the United States and most of them fail, but some don't and hope springs eternal."*

I was honored to meet George Shultz in his office on the Stanford University campus where he was, once again, in the middle of writing the next article and the next book.

Foreigners in Silicon Valley

I had an interesting conversation a few years ago with Mr. Lee Kuan Yew, the man who developed Singapore and who is an extraordinarily able person. Singapore was in the process of establishing a venture fund of some kind here in the U.S. I asked him why he was doing that and he said that Singapore was realizing that they had to sort of loosen up a little and they needed people who were more creative.

He thought this, the U.S., was the place to get exposed to this. I said, "Well you know there are people from all over the world here. This isn't just U.S. people here." He said, "I know that." I said, "Maybe you could do this just anywhere," and he said, "No, it couldn't be just anywhere. Only in this country [the U.S.] could this kind of talent get assembled, because of the peculiar welcoming and nurturing atmosphere." Because, he said, "It seems like in Silicon Valley all they care about is that you're very smart and that you're willing to work 24 hours a day, forever." And that's it—nationality doesn't mean a thing.

I thought it was a very interesting comment.

Q: *What factors make Silicon Valley so unique?*

A: The willingness to let people fail is very important because it gives flexibility to the economy. There are something like 600,000 new enterprises started each year in the United States and most of them fail, but some don't and hope springs eternal. It's also true that big companies are allowed to fail here in the U.S. In most countries, that's harder, but if you take a Fortune 500 in, say,1960, ask yourself how many of those companies are left in the 1990s? Less than half are still there. We had a few bailouts as in Chrysler and Lockheed but by and large, the United States lets competition sort people out.

Leadership

Q: *What are the most important things to keep in mind to be a good leader?*

A: I've always felt in my own career, whether in the university where I was a dean, or in a company or in the various government posts I've had, that if you could create an atmosphere around you where everybody is learning, you're going to have a good group. People like to learn, so that atmosphere to me is one of the keys to giving leadership to people. People are developing themselves as well as whatever they're working on.

Q: *What about multicultural leadership?*

A: It's a much more mobile scene here and to a certain degree elsewhere, you have to be mobile, that's true.

Of course you have to understand other cultures. And we've worked on that reasonably well in this country but it's easy to get lazy here because so much of the world now operates in English.

This is a big country—if you lived in Belgium, say, you'd know you have to speak Flemish and French; otherwise you wouldn't be able to operate at all. Something different has happened in the last few decades. When I was in business in Bechtel, we had lots of work overseas and at Bechtel, we all learned when you go to another country and operate there, you have to learn how to hire people, live with people, buy things, sell things, and Bechtel was good at that.

But I said to them, "Now it's different doing international business, we now live in a more global environment." That means if you never leave Peoria, you're part of the global environment and you better understand what's going on—or try to. Besides, the whole world has shifted its views in that sense.

Hiring Overseas

Q: *Don't companies nowadays hire local managers overseas to do the hiring and firing?*

A: We had to hire local people for many reasons, because it was less expensive there, for example. But you had certain standards and you'd do better with a U.S. person who understands the standards until the others learned. There are rules in the United States that are much more extensive than in most other countries, about what we call, for example, bribery.

Advice

Q: *What advice would you give to young foreign professionals living or coming here?*

A: Well, do interesting things, work hard, and if you find yourself at a dead end, move. Be mobile.

Foreigners' Contributions to Silicon Valley

Q: *How do you think Silicon Valley has changed due to foreign-born professionals' contributions?*

A: It got more creative. People had different ways of looking at things. People who come are extraordinarily able and bring tremendous capabilities.

It's somewhat a self-selecting process. They come here and if they're not able to operate, they leave. And people are looking not for foreign contributions, they're looking for contributions and it turns out that some people who really contributed come from another country.

Talent going Elsewhere

Q: *Do you think the window of opportunity has closed here—with the limits on H-1B visas?*

A: It's a problem getting the right balance with the visas. Between your concern for security and your readiness to have people come, who are wanted, I think our whole immigration laws need a fundamental review, not just the Mexican illegal-type problem. I hope that comes one of these days.

U.S.—The Next 20 Years

Q: *Where do you see the U.S. in the next 20 years—as an economic power versus China or India?*

A: The United States will still be a dominant economy by a mile. First of all, we're much bigger to begin with and a very high proportion of what is created in the economy originates in the United States—and Silicon Valley is a prime example. We are strong in the whole biotech business, we're a leader in that.

We're also a strong financial leader, we have a system that is probably more flexible than that of most other countries. That means that more change will happen here and also more easily.

People resist people who complain about globalization and that it is causing the change, but willingness to change and the pattern of change has been a constant here.

Probably part of the process of moving forward is the willingness to change. China is growing so fast because it's adding to its labor force by pulling people into the cities and because it is sort of leapfrogging in technology; it is able to use the technology that we have developed and that causes their products to rise; as they catch up, they become users of modern technology. That means they're going to have to work on the cutting edge, which they don't have to do right now.

Eric Schmidt, Chairman and CEO, Google, written statement

Eric Schmidt
Chairman and CEO, Google
Country of Origin: U.S.
Group: The American Hosts

> *"Silicon Valley itself is a better, dynamic and more credible place because of the contributions of immigrants from outside the United States."*

Eric's written response on the role that foreign-born entrepreneurs have played in the Silicon Valley:

"Executives and entrepreneurs from outside the United States have been critical to the rise and continued success of Silicon Valley. One of Google's founders, in fact, was born in Russia.

Technology is fundamentally a global business—and only increasingly so with the growth of the Internet. The perspectives offered by professionals from outside the U.S. have and will continue to inform important decisions made by Silicon Valley-based multinationals.

In businesses like Google's, we are quickly realizing that one size doesn't fit all; indeed, our U.S.-based products and services—available everywhere because of the Internet—must still be localized and refined to meet the needs of most of the world's people.

We at Google are squarely focused on the internationalization of our business and thus constantly rely on the skills, perspectives and judgment of our foreign-born executives and colleagues.

Silicon Valley itself is a better, dynamic and more credible place because of the contributions of immigrants from outside the United States."

Scott McNealy, Chairman and Co-Founder, Sun Microsystems, written statement

Scott McNealy
Chairman and Co-Founder, Sun Microsystems
Country of Origin: U.S.
Group: The American Hosts

> *"The economic, global and social benefits to getting everyone in the world connected are endless."*

Scott was so busy at the time I met him at a Stanford breakfast event, that he could only agree to answer a few questions in writing.

Q: *Which foreign execs stand out in your mind who have made a significant difference/contribution in SV?*

A: Vinod Khosla and Andy Bechtolsheim, two of Sun's co-founders, have made significant contributions not only to Silicon Valley, but also to the technology industry at large.

Java, created by Canadian-born James Gosling, is but one example of the contributions Sun made in the past 25 years.

Q: *In your opinion, has the window of opportunity closed in Silicon Valley as many people overseas think—in light of foreign professionals going back to China and India and using the better educated engineers there to build start-ups?*

A: At Sun, our strategy is to open source our technology. The beauty of this strategy is that it is geography blind. It lets us find talent anywhere in the world, it lets us conduct R&D anywhere in the world, it lets us work with customers (including start-ups) that are based anywhere in the world. It lets us continue to be mavericks, to continue to push the envelope of innovation. I think it's a good thing that countries around the world are working to create a Silicon Valley-like atmosphere: we will all benefit from this.

Q: *What did foreign professionals do differently here in the Valley than Americans would have done or did?*

A: I won't speculate on what they would have done (or still do) differently, but I can talk about what resources are in Silicon Valley that Sun and others take advantage of on a regular basis. Silicon Valley has top universities and research facilities—both of which closely work with the private industry to drive innovation. Sun, which stands for Stanford University Network, was started at Stanford.

There's also a critical mass of support organizations and infrastructure here, from law firms to banks to venture capitalists. And, finally, we have great weather, which makes this an appealing place to live and work.

Vinton Cerf, Chief Internet Evangelist, Google

Vinton Cerf
Chief Internet Evangelist, Google
Country of Origin: U.S.
Group: The American Hosts

> *"There will probably be more things on the Internet than people. By the time we get to 2010, it's conceivable that there will be as many as two or three billion users and maybe six billion devices."*

Vinton Cerf is a giant among the greats of Silicon Valley; yet he's one of the most approachable and helpful individuals I have ever met.

Q: *How would you describe what you are doing professionally today?*

A: Well, I think my title at Google comes close to it; I am the "Chief Internet Evangelist." For all practical purposes I have been evangelizing the spread of the Internet since its beginning, so I continue to do that. I also spend a lot of time trying to deal with Internet policy, which turned out to be an extremely complex matter.

Q: *How did your childhood experiences or your family influence your choice of careers?*

A: My family had a pretty strong influence in some respects; my mother and father were both very strong advocates of education and so they encouraged me to read a lot. My mother played classical music with me and we played games trying to guess which composer it was. My father was a Phi Beta Kappa. They both had college graduate degrees. When I was interested in chemistry, they got me chemistry sets. In mechanical matters, I got the predecessors to LEGOs, you know, Erector Sets, made out of metal parts.

So the family house was filled with books, there was a lot of political debate and other kinds of discussions over the dinner table.

Q: *Where were you raised?*

A: I was born in New Haven, Connecticut. When the war was over, we moved to Los Angeles and I grew up in the suburbs of L.A., in the San Fernando Valley. I basically spent the first 18 years, for all practical purposes, in the San Fernando Valley and then ping-ponged back and forth from the Stanford four-year undergraduate work to Southern California where I worked during the summer.

Advanced Degrees

Q: *And then you chose UCLA.*

A: Well, before I chose UCLA, after I graduated from Stanford, I came to L.A. to work for IBM. I worked for IBM for a couple of years and realized that I really needed an advanced degree because I needed to know more about the computers I was working with. I enrolled in the graduate program at UCLA in 1967 and spent five years working on a Master's and Ph.D.

After I finished at UCLA, I went up to Stanford to teach. I joined the faculty in teaching and research, and of course that's where the concept of the Internet was born, together with Bob Kahn who was at that time in the Defense Advanced Project Agency in Washington D.C.

Biggest Obstacles

Q: *What were some of the biggest obstacles you had to overcome in your career, whether in your job or in education?*

A: I didn't feel obstacles as a student. I also won't say I breezed through school. I did well in high school, but I did less well at Stanford where the competition was tougher. I am hearing impaired, though. That was a challenge. I was not deaf and I wasn't born deaf. I was born with almost normal hearing, but by the time I was 13, I began wearing hearing aids. I have been wearing hearing aids for over 50 years now. Of course, as my hearing has gotten worse, the hearing aids have gotten better, fortunately. I have been able to function pretty much in a hearing world, despite a fairly severe loss.

Getting the Internet Set Up

Q: *What about obstacles in your profession?*

A: What's probably been the most challenging thing is fighting the technical battles. It was an uphill battle to get people to accept the ARPANET. For ten years, I fought the battle to get the government to accept the idea that TCP/IP was at least as good if not better than OSI. That went on probably from about 1985 to, let's say, 1993. Now, of course, the Internet is widespread, although it only has a billion users, so we have 5-1/2 billion to go.

Success

Q: *What is your definition of being successful?*

A: Success to me means doing something that makes a difference. It seems to me that it could be a small thing or a big thing. It doesn't matter how big it is; it only matters if it makes a difference. It could be doing something for a person in your family. It could be doing something for a person you don't know. It could be something that affects millions of people.

Foreign Influences

Q: *Another question which leads me to foreign influences, how do you think Silicon Valley changed due to foreign-born professionals coming here?*

A: First of all our graduate schools have benefited for years with some of the brightest minds in the world coming to study and do research here. That has been a positive thing for both our own research institutions and for those individuals.

There is one segment that has been wildly successful on average and that's our Indian population. The Asian population similarly: very focused on education and their professional development. Many of those individuals have also gone on to have quite an impact in our industry. The most impressive is the Indian population that came here, studied here, and then began to learn how to outsource some of the work to back home, to India.

This has been a good thing for a lot of people because it certainly gave jobs to people in India without having them leave the country. It provided low cost and high quality services although there is tension because of the argument that the jobs are being outsourced and it's a bad thing for the U.S. I think it's a replay of what happened in the manufacturing industry, when manufacturing went to where the costs are lower. You can't argue with that.

Q: *What do you think foreign professionals do differently in the Silicon Valley than Americans?*

A: Well, it's my impression of many of the foreign professionals that they work harder. And this isn't to say that there aren't people in the U.S. who work hard—there are—and at the top levels they are all equally good. On average, we see a very, very high level of performance coming from foreign-born professionals. One of the side effects is the professionals who make it into this country. The quality is extremely high, so you can expect that the people who make it here to study are the cream of the crop.

Q: *Which people come to mind who were really successful in the Silicon Valley and who are foreign-born? Besides the obvious Yahoo! and Google?*

Good heavens, how about Vinod Khosla [Co-Founder of Sun Microsystems], how about the former head of Intel, Andy Grove? I also have former students who have done extremely well, although they aren't as visible to the public. Yogen Dalal from India was my student. He went off and did some wonderful things at Xerox PARC and then at Apple. He became one of the principals in the venture capital company called Mayfield Associates.

Advice to Foreign-Born Professionals

Q: *What advice would you give Indian, Chinese or French young professionals who live here or come here to work? What is really important to know?*

A: Probably the most important thing is to assimilate as much as possible, in my view. The historical melting pot in the United States basically said that if you apply yourself, if you learn English, blend into the population, apply yourself and work hard, that almost anything is possible. I would say that many, many of the people who come here, whether they come here as graduate students or contemporary professionals, or perhaps they just come here to start small businesses—many of them have followed that course.

Success in Silicon Valley

Q: *What do you think it takes to be successful in the Silicon Valley?*

A: Well, several things. First of all a willingness to take risk, second a willingness to risk failure. Let me give you an interesting quote. When several of us met with Tony Blair a few weeks ago at Cisco headquarters, John Chambers hosted the meeting; it was a couple of hours' lunch affair. We had Steve Jobs and Hector Ruiz from AMD and Jonathan Schwartz from Sun Microsystems. There were maybe ten of us from the Valley area. Tony was interested to see if it was possible to replicate the Silicon Valley in London.

So I thought an interesting way to start would be to ask the various assembled representatives from our industry what it was about the Silicon Valley that had contributed to their success. Steve Jobs gets up and says, "One of the interesting things we have in common is that we have all failed at one time or another."

He said, “However, in Europe it’s a different matter, if you fail, you’re dead, and you might as well be wearing a scarlet letter on your sleeve.”

So there is tolerance for failure in the Silicon Valley, as long as you don’t fail at everything. We treat that as an experience as opposed to failure, if there aren’t too many of them.

Second, there is an availability of capital in the Silicon Valley that you don’t have elsewhere.

Third, we have sources of very, very smart people coming out of Berkeley, Stanford and San Jose State and so on, both on the technical side particularly and in the business world. And, there is a sociological element to it. It’s a small place. A lot of us know each other.

We worked for one another at one time or the other, we have competed, we have cooperated. There is a social network in the Valley which is much looser than a Japanese “keiretsu” but it is a closer community than you typically get in places like London.

The more I see of all this, the more I am persuaded that it’s the people that you hire—that is more important than anything. It is more important to hire really good, smart people who fit in really well to a certain style than it is to hire precisely for a particular job. It is important to have really, really good people and tailor the jobs, than not have such good people who are only theoretically matched to a particular job.

International Background or Experience?

Q: *Do you think it is important to hire people with an international background?*

A: I think it is vital to have people with international experience. There are two reasons for that: one of them is the general globalization that is going on, where the probability you are working with colleagues who are from a different culture, a different country, different languages, is very high.

There is a second reason for hiring people with an international outlook and that is that the businesses, the products and the services may have to be international to sustain the business. It may not be a purely domestic business. It gives you a functioning sustainable company. The best examples of that are in countries that have a small population. The best examples of that are the northern countries—Sweden, Norway, and so on; or the island countries like New Zealand, where information technology may not be sustainable strictly within the domestic market. Therefore you have to tailor that product and service to a much broader base. You need to understand the culture, the business atmosphere and the business practices, and people outside your domestic environment or you won't be successful.

Future Growth of the Internet

Q: *Since you are really the original creator of the Internet, I can ask you this: Where do you think the Internet is going to go now?*

It's going to continue to grow. We passed what we think is the billion user mark in the Internet world. What we've seen in the last few years is an absolutely explosive growth in mobile communication, which is increasingly linked to the Internet and therefore affecting it.

In particular, things people are interested in because they are using mobile equipment have emphasized the utility of geographically indexed information. People want to know: what is near where I am, where can I go, what can I do, where is the nearest ATM machine, where is the nearest hospital, what things are of interest nearby, how do I get there from here?

There is increasing broadband access in the fixed environment, including fiber to the premises whether it's business or in the home. That will, of course, introduce some very interesting entertainment opportunities that depend on *the long tail*. The fact that the storage and transmission are potentially extremely cheap means that people's entertainment behavior will shift away from watching videos while they are being transmitted, which we typically see today in the cable television world or satellite to downloading and playing back, which is more an iPod-style thing.

I predict that more of the entertainment will be under the control of the consumer rather than under the control of the programmer.

Wild Future Projections

Q: *How about some wild projections where you think this all might also go?*

A: Well, I should also emphasize that I think we will have our interplanetary extension in operation by the end of the decade, so that's strictly in support of research programs.

The wildest observation is that there will probably be more things on the Internet than people. By the time we get to 2010, it's conceivable that there will be as many as two or three billion users and maybe six billion devices. You already are almost there. If you have an Internet-enabled car, if you have any Internet-enabled appliances at home, if you have any Internet-enabled Internet appliances at the office and if you carry anything around, like a laptop or a PDA or anything mobile that's Internet-enabled, you are already there.

Q: *How does it make you feel to know that you have been a major contributor to this equalization tool, which has brought the world closer and has given many people a chance to live differently?*

A: Well first of all, my role in this is sort of very basic. I think of myself as having provided the plumbing, or if you want to put it another way, having figured out how to build highways.

Everybody else has figured out what businesses to put on the highways, what cars and automobiles and trucks to put on the highway. I didn't do any of that. I am happy to have created an environment or helped to create an environment in which that kind of innovation has been both stimulated and rewarded. I feel compelled to remind you and others that the real credit goes to the people who figured out how to use this technology in ways that have proven beneficial.

Steve Westly, Founder and CEO, The Westly Group

Steve Westly
Founder and CEO, The Westly Group,
Former California State Controller
Country of Origin: U.S.
Group: The American Hosts

> *"So it's basically: take a risk, shoot high."*

Steve was my student in Spanish when I was a Teaching Assistant at Stanford University during my Ph.D. studies. I had fun working with him again on his Spanish in preparation for his election as Controller for the State of California.

Childhood Influences

Q: *How did your childhood experiences and your family influence your choice of careers?*

A: Going into politics was a shock to my family. No one in my family had ever gone into politics or government. But, my parents always tried to give me a sense that I could change the world. They just hoped that it would be in the private sector. My father always taught me about international affairs and the world around us because he grew up in the Philippines, fought in a World War and had traveled all around the world. I think that is part of what got me thinking about government and politics at an early age. My parents did get me interested in government and the world around us.

Education

Q: *What role did your education play in what you are currently doing or in your future plans?*

A: I was a History major at Stanford. I think that helped broaden and ground me for going into government. Having an MBA also helped me to be successful in the private sector.

What does Success Mean to You?

Q: *Tell me what it means to you to be successful.*

A: For me it's a combination. For me it is balance, it is doing good in the world and helping people. Also, it means being a good father, a good parent. There is the external part of helping people and the internal part of being a good husband and father. Then there is something bigger than that: being a good custodian for the planet. Something we are not doing so well right now.

I'm always looking for the next new thing. As I go forward, I'd like to use some of my skills, contacts and experiences to help make the world a better place [which he did in 2007 by founding his new company, The Westly Group]. After my term as Controller ends, I will go back into the private sector to work on building Clean Technology companies that I hope will change the world.

Role of Silicon Valley

Q: *Could you have been successful outside of Silicon Valley or did this environment give you something you could get nowhere else?*

A: Silicon Valley is a very special place. I think it has enabled me to do things I couldn't have done anywhere else in the world.

Because people here are taught to think big, they are taught to think out of the box, they are taught to take risks and they are taught to tolerate failure. I think there's much less tolerance for failing in other countries. That can stifle innovation and risk-taking.

Multicultural Leadership Today

Q: *What are the greatest challenges in your opinion in multicultural leadership today?*

A: Multicultural leadership requires totally different skill sets and I think that our schools have traditionally not done a good job at teaching that. America has been very self-centered. Our executives need to learn more about other countries and cultures, to be more tolerant and most of all, respectful.

I'd hate to see how far down Americans rank in terms of what they call not only geographical understanding, but also multicultural understanding. We need to dramatically improve geographic awareness in our schools.

Important Leadership Skills

Q: *What are the three most important things you have to know nowadays being a leader?*

A: It's a very, very good question. First, I think you have to understand the situation before acting. We didn't do a very good job of this in Iraq.

Second, I think you need to be an effective communicator.

And third, I would say is to move quickly. If there's anything that I have seen change in my life, it's that victory goes not to people who move the most quickly, nor does it go necessarily to the smartest—but to the people who have a clear vision and who execute on it the most quickly. At eBay, we made a lot of mistakes, but nobody moved as quickly as we did.

Foreign Contributions to Silicon Valley

Q: *How do you think Silicon Valley changed due to foreign professionals' contributions?*

A: It wouldn't be Silicon Valley without foreign professionals. Most of the success stories are from immigrants and foreign professionals. Over half the companies that go public in Silicon Valley are taken public by foreign professionals. This is what makes Silicon Valley the most dynamic place in the world.

Q: *What do you think foreign professionals do differently than the Americans do, or did?*

A: I think there are two things going on, we attract the best and the brightest from all over the world, you included; they come to our educational institutions and they stay. Secondly, they tend to be hungrier and work harder.

Mentoring

Q: *If you were to mentor foreign professionals how would you do it differently than if you were mentoring American professionals?*

A: My first comment is that they should be mentoring me, these people have a lot to teach us.

Second, for the foreign professionals that come here, they need to learn to speak English well. You can go abroad and get by speaking English in many countries. It's very difficult to get by without speaking English here. If you don't speak English well or have a strong accent, it's harder.

Q: *What advice would you give foreigners who want to come here to work?*

A: The main thing is to not be afraid to take risks. Foreign professionals come here and they are often tremendously well educated. The ones that you see succeed are the ones that step it up and take risks.

So it's basically: take a risk, shoot high. Many of the engineers who come here are not necessarily smarter than the ones who stay home, but by virtue of their coming here, they have shown that they're willing to take a risk and make a sacrifice.

Guy Kawasaki, Managing Director, Garage Technology Ventures

Guy Kawasaki
Managing Director, Garage Technology Ventures
Country of Origin: U.S.
Group: The American Hosts

> *"Immigrants are a source of the renewal of entrepreneurship and hunger and without that we would be stuck."*

Guy Kawasaki's irreverence and humor cuts straight to the issue whenever he speaks or writes. His blog is a must read for insights into Silicon Valley.

Q: *What are you doing professionally today?*

A: I am a venture capitalist and a managing director at Garage Technology Ventures, an early stage venture firm in Palo Alto, California. That's my day job. I also give about 100 speeches a year, and I have a very active blog.

Childhood

Q: *How did your childhood experiences and your upbringing contribute to where you are today?*

A: If you're looking for the great story where at eight years old I had a lemonade stand and all that crap, there was none of that. I had a very normal childhood—a middle class family, nothing special. My father was a fireman, became a real estate broker, and then he became a state senator. I don't come from money, but I'm not a boat person who comes from total poverty either.

Obstacles

Q: *What are some of the biggest obstacles you had to overcome to be where you are today?*

A: Certainly race has never been an obstacle. I am from Hawaii, and the Japanese ran Hawaii when I was growing up, so I never felt oppressed. Japanese Americans from California or the Mainland may have this feeling, but I don't.

I came to the Mainland to go to Stanford. After Stanford, I went to law school because my parents wanted me to. I hated it so I dropped out after two weeks, and I went back home for six months. But I came back and got an MBA from UCLA. Then I went to work for a jewelry company. I did very well in the jewelry business, but I fell in love with computers and went to Apple and the rest is history.

What is Success?

Q: *What is success for you?*

A: If there were a mantra for me, it would be, "empower entrepreneurs." I try to empower entrepreneurs through my writing, through my speaking and through my funding. I don't want to be an entrepreneur. I empower entrepreneurs.

Q: *But in a way, you are an entrepreneur.*

A: Not really, I don't consider myself successful as an entrepreneur. I'm not Larry Ellison or Bill Gates or Steve Jobs. They are successful entrepreneurs. I have four children and a wife, and they are more important than my profession. The other thing that drives me is that I love ice hockey. If I spent as much time writing as I do playing hockey, I'd win a Pulitzer Prize.

Q: *Could you have been as successful as you are here outside of the Silicon Valley?*

A: This is a hard question to answer. If you took a Steve Jobs or a Bill Gates and you stuck them in the middle of Africa, they would still be where they are today. I guess if I were in a place that was anti-entrepreneurship, rigid and controlling, I probably would have left.

Q: *What are the greatest challenges for multicultural leadership that you see today?*

A: I am what I am. Maybe if I were in Europe, I would tailor my message slightly. I think that people in Europe are too focused on their family's past. For example, in France you meet people who say my uncle's cousin's second nephew was Napoleon's lieutenant and for that reason I'm special. I couldn't care less. I don't care if you are Bill Gates' son, much less Napoleon's uncle's second cousin's cousin.

The other side of it is, if you fail in your current life in some countries, it seems your family has to bear that burden for the next five hundred years. I don't get that at all.

Contributions to the Valley

Q: *How do you think Silicon Valley changed because of the contribution of the foreign-born professionals here?*

A: Okay, the Valley started in the thirties, let's say, with Hewlett and Packard and Fairchild and all that. By now, this is some 70-odd years later. It would be Packard's son and his son's son running the Valley. So they are rich and they might not have the same edge.

Suppose we had stopped people from coming to America in 1993 by sealing off the borders. America would suck today if this had been done. Immigrants are a source of the renewal of entrepreneurship and hunger and without that we would be stuck.

Q: *Can you give me a short time line and tell me who influenced what development? What nationality contributed to what things in high tech?*

A: Naturally, the white people made the first chips and semiconductors, no question. That was in the '30s and '40s. But soon the Indians and Chinese made massive contributions. It's not that clear that you can pick the culture and say when they came.

One thing you can clearly say is that it's not third- or fourth-generation Anglos who are doing it.

Q: *If you were going to teach something at a boot camp for entrepreneurs in the Valley, what would you teach American professionals and what would you teach foreign-born professionals?*

A: A broad generalization is that Americans need to learn about engineering and foreigners need to learn about marketing. The ideal combination is that the Anglo is doing marketing, the Chinese is doing finance, and the Indian is doing engineering. [laughter]

Foreign Contributors

Q: *Which foreign executives stand out in your mind who have made a really significant contribution in Silicon Valley?*

A: Vinod Khosla [Sun Microsystems, Khosla Ventures], Pierre Omidiyar [eBay], and Suhas Patil [Cirrus Logic] are good examples. Andy Grove [Intel], too.

Do Backgrounds Count Here?

Q: *Do you consider people's background when you think of what they do professionally or does it disappear here in Silicon Valley?*

A: I have a previous disposition towards liking Indian entrepreneurs. I think they work harder and they are smarter. You can almost make a case in America, the thicker and the worse the accent, the richer the person is.

Q: *Maybe, outside of California?*

A: Inside California. The immigrants are rich here. My sweet spot is to find two Indians who are quitting a Stanford Ph.D. Computer Science degree. That's the richest vein. The worst vein is an Anglo who is second- or third-generation rich.

Q: *Do you think the Silicon Valley will continue to be successful?*

A: I think in the foreseeable future, call that 10 or 20 years, this place will still be, for cultural reasons, for legal reasons, for whatever, this will still be *the* place. Yes, China will be a great market but in China you never know when you really own anything, unless you are the premier's brother-in-law. A lot of Indians come here and make a lot of money and then they go back to India.

Innovation

Q: *Does the U.S. still have the fertile ground for innovation?*

A: We certainly have. I don't know if China does. I hesitate to say that it will just clean our clock, but I certainly think it could.

Nat Goldhaber, Managing Director, Claremont Creek Ventures

Nat Goldhaber
Managing Director, Claremont Creek Ventures
Country of Origin: U.S.
Group: The American Hosts

> *"I think it is the absolute complete, unfettered social mobility that is possible, so with certain very limited constraints, you are what you can achieve. Period!"*

Nat was kind enough to talk to me on the phone. I had come to know of him through Randy Hawks, a fellow VC, who assured me that hearing Nat's story was a must.

Q: *Tell me what you are doing now.*

A: I am a managing director of a venture capital fund, Claremont Creek Ventures, an early stage venture fund.

Childhood Influences

Q: *How did your childhood and your education influence where you are today?*

A: I come from a family of scientists. My mother, my father, my uncle, and my aunt and cousins are all physicists. My father was awarded California Scientist of the Year for his groundbreaking work in the discovery of a quark called "Charm." More recently, he was the discoverer of the phenomenon known as "Dark Energy," perhaps the most important discovery in Physics in the last half of the 20th century.

I've done some major work in a variety of different areas. I grew up hearing physics at home; it was a deeply scientific household. It was not uncommon for us to have more than one Nobel Prize winner over for Friday night dinners.

University Studies

Q: *So what did you end up studying?*

A: I have a Master's Degree from UC Berkeley in Education. During my studies at Berkeley, I spent my time with Maharishi Mahesh Yogi, founder of Transcendental Meditation. I became interested in Transcendental Mediation and spent years founding and operating his organization in the U.S. and elsewhere.

TM Origins

Q: *Really? How did you get involved with that?*

A: When I was 17, long before the before the Beatles popularized TM, I found out about it on a trip with my parents. My parents were on a lecture tour around the world, talking about physics, and they took me along.

When I was at Oxford, my mother introduced me to a physicist named Dr. Matts Roos. He told me all about transcendental meditation and I started practicing TM in London. Then, I went on after that to India with my parents and met the Maharishi for the first time in 1965. Pretty much the next ten years, until 1975, I was working full time for Maharishi.

Q: *What did you pursue afterwards?*

A: On and off, from then on, I'd do a semester or two of college and then I'd stop and do full time teaching of transcendental meditation or running the TM center, or running off and spending six months with Maharishi somewhere in the world.

For the next ten years, more of less, this was a career. I didn't really return to school again full time until 1975, when I came back to UC Berkeley to get a Master's Degree in Education.

Politics

Then about three-quarters of the way through, just about at the Master's Degree level, a good friend of mine, Bill Scranton, was running for Lt. Gov. of Pennsylvania. He invited me back to Pennsylvania to ride around in the car with him for the last few weeks of the campaign and he won. He then asked me to be his Chief of Staff.

So I went back to Pennsylvania, with my wife-to-be, and we lived there for five years. My first job there was Director of the Governor's Energy Council. About three months into our administration, the Three Mile Island accident happened.

First Start-Up Companies

When I ended my stint in politics I started my first company, which was called, interestingly enough, "The Web" long before there was one.

It was a local area networking system for the CP/M operating system. Then I moved to California and started a new company which was called TOPS, which stands for transcendental operating system. That was quite a big success. I sold it to Sun Microsystems in 1987 and became a VP of Sun.

I did my first stint as venture capitalist a year later. I left Sun; the venture fund that had funded TOPS invited me to be a partner.

After that, I started a company which I took public which was called Cybergold, it was one of the very early online direct marketing companies. Then we merged with another company called MyPoints and ultimately sold the combined entity to United Airlines where it's still operating.

Running for Vice President of these United States

Then I ran for Vice President of the United States. The day that I merged my company with MyPoints, I went to the Reform Party Convention in Long Beach and ended up as candidate for Vice President.

Q: *Was this with Ross Perot?*

A: No, it was the election after he had backed out. It was the year of the big hullabaloo between the Ross Perot guard of the Reform Party and Pat Buchanan. The Reform Party split in two—we were part of the splinter group. John Hagelin and I were the standard bearers for that splinter group.

Skills needed for Success

Q: *What skills do you think one must have to be successful today, say in the high-tech area?*

A: Well, as hackneyed as it sounds, it means to be able to think expansively; you need to be able to aggregate existing pieces, predict new developments, and combine those pieces in ways that are completely unusual and novel.

That is what you need to be successful at any time and in any field. It is no more or no less true today. The difference is that the pieces are popping up much more rapidly than ever before in human history; probably a thousandfold from what it was at the turn of the century, and a millionfold or ten millionfold what it was in the early eighteen hundreds, not to mention the Stone Age.

I think that if there is more, it requires a kind of level of nimbleness and willingness to respond rapidly to extremely rapid changes and to be able to understand. The best way to describe it is by taking a step back from the fray; you are able to observe what is taking place and understand how the assembly of the pieces can have meaningful effects.

Changes in Silicon Valley

Q: *So how do you think Silicon Valley changed due to the influences of foreign professionals?*

A: I think there are two answers to that question. First, the excitement and dynamism of the area has attracted and continues to attract the best and the brightest from around the world; so the foreign nationals that are coming to work here tended to be absolutely the top of the pack. We have drained the finest brains; that is sort of step one.

Second, there are ways in which you can understand the world that are impossible in one cultural milieu and not another. There may be insights that occur that are simply impossible to have, if you don't have the kind of cultural background and possibilities. In a very Heideggerian way, you can't be other than what you are, and what you are is informed by where you came from. The old expression we used to use in the '60s, "It's where you're at." It's not your physical location, "It's where you're *at*."

Uniqueness of Silicon Valley

Q: *What is unique about Silicon Valley?*

I think it is the absolute complete, unfettered social mobility that is possible. So with certain very mild constraints, you are what you can achieve. Period!

An individual's ability to rise here is completely independent of historical background, cultural background, national background, religion. That's really why this has all happened here, and not, for example in Boston, which still has a very strong class consciousness.

Here, you go to a restaurant and the waiter that you are talking to you treat in the same way that you would treat someone whom you might expect someday to be a millionaire. That is absolutely not the case anywhere else in the world. It's not true in New York. It's not true in Hollywood. You're either a movie star or a waiter and if you are a waiter, probably you are never going to be a movie star.

Challenges for Multicultural Leadership

Q: *What would you say are the greatest challenges for multicultural leadership today; especially for an American executive working with other cultures and overseas?*

A: I am not sure that conditions today are that different today than they ever were. I think an American leader running a foreign team in a foreign land probably has more or less the same things to worry about as he or she did in the past, namely being respectful of practices and having a lot of patience especially in those areas where the practices are significantly different.

India and China

What I think has changed in India and China for the first time ever, is that there is genuine "Silicon Valley style entrepreneurship" emerging.

India, of course, has this gigantic hangover of the caste system where the development of a true meritocracy is difficult, vis-à-vis raising capital, the ability to hire employees, the ability to be respected as a manager when you are not from the right caste.

The allure of entrepreneurship is very significant with this enormous change going on in both China and India today; India, with a middle class now, is larger than the population of the United States. It's a first for India. Unless you go back to mythical Vedic times, it's probably the first time in all of India's history that there has been such pervasive wealth. I'm sure it's the same in China.

I think it's wonderful, it's absolutely terrific. There are people who believe that ancient Vedic traditions are being completely forgotten in favor of the allure of Western behavior. My vantage point is that it's a hell of a lot better to have people well off and enjoying life than having them suffering and impoverished.

The other good news is the Internet, because we now have a frictionless and essentially free communication. You can now begin to bypass the sluggish, lethargic bureaucracy, and the lethargic caste system and connect directly with nodes of excellence, which are actually the human beings who are rising to the top.

So on the worldwide Internet, you basically achieve a global meritocracy. It's entirely independent of the constraints that might be imposed because of lingering discrimination based upon race, creed, color, family background, wealth, etc. This is extremely good news for everyone in the world.

Although, particularly here in the Valley, we will no longer be as much the center of the universe as far as creativity and innovation are concerned, we instead will get a great benefit on the other side: the creation of a global meritocracy, where frictionlessly, you can connect people, even on an ad hoc basis, to create new products, new ideas independent of where they live, and of their historical background. That's extremely good news. I have to say we are not there yet, but also that is not very far away.

Chapter

11 Conclusion

Lessons from Successful Foreign-Born Entrepreneurs

While some of you might see these interviews as anecdotal, as random thoughts of 38 individuals with whom I spent a short amount of time, the lessons I draw from their stories are congruent with broader studies.

In an important 2006 survey of 340 privately-held, venture-backed companies, Anderson and Platzer highlight the fact that, "Immigrant entrepreneurs and professionals contribute significantly to job creation and innovation in the United States. This analysis shows the striking propensity of immigrants to start and grow successful American companies, particularly in the technology field. The study's findings reflect the benefits of an open policy toward legal immigration." [16]

---

16. Anderson, S. and M. Platzer, *American Made: The Impact of Immigrant Entrepreneurs and Professionals on U.S. Competitiveness*, National Venture Capital Association (NVCA), 2006.

Their findings include:

- Over the past 15 years, immigrants have started 25 percent of U.S. public companies that were venture-backed, a high percentage of the most innovative companies in America.
- The current market capitalization of publicly traded immigrant-founded venture-backed companies in the United States exceeds $500 billion.
- Forty percent of U.S. publicly traded venture-backed companies operating in high-technology manufacturing today were started by immigrants.
- Immigrants possess great entrepreneurial capacity, particularly in technical fields.
- The proportion of immigrant entrepreneurs among publicly traded venture-backed companies is particularly impressive when compared to entrepreneurs in the general U.S. population.
- Immigrant-founded venture-backed public companies today employ an estimated 220,000 people in the United States.

Lessons Learned

I believe that my interviews show in detail why findings from this larger survey hold true for the individuals I talked to. A unique mix of characteristics shows up time and again in the interviews, which showcase the ability of immigrants to succeed in Silicon Valley and the U.S. in general.

Consider some of these characteristics, which stand out in the interviews. The people I talked with all exhibit:

- High intelligence, often coupled with a great educational background
- A willingness to work hard, focus, determination and perseverance
- A vision for success in their professional careers and personal lives

- Curiosity and passion
- Love of family and a dedication to supporting it
- An often uncanny insight into themselves and others
- Belief in themselves
- Openness to emotional and intellectual growth
- A tolerance for, even a love of, risk and the ability to (quickly) recover from failure
- An appetite to collaborate
- Humility
- A desire to give back to society

Now ask yourself, how many of these characteristics are found in a typical cross-section of the native-born population of, say, Boston, Massachusetts? Not many regions of the U.S. have whole populations who share these characteristics. But, I would say the same is true of a typical cross-section of Bristol, England; Bangalore, India; or Berlin, Germany. By setting out on their journey to Silicon Valley or other parts of the U.S., the people I spoke with are a self-selecting sample. They are anything but typical.

Recipes for Success

Each person in this book tells a unique story. But the characteristics they have as a group are a wonderful "shopping list" for anyone looking to succeed in Silicon Valley. Bear in mind that there is no "secret sauce" that guarantees your success. But there are a number of "recipes for success" with ingredients that the people I met have used to their advantage. If you plan to immigrate to the U.S. and establish yourself in Silicon Valley, you should know that it is the extraordinary, not the ordinary, who succeed. With that in mind, consider some of the extraordinary aspects of the people I interviewed. Here are some recipes for success, which you might find, will work for you.

First Recipe: Stand Out from the Crowd

"You come to this country to prove something to yourself, to really do the best you can in your education, the best you can in your profession, build a life and be successful. I really think it's this sense of energy. I think of it as: you are successful when you get up in the morning, you're really passionate about what you are doing, and you really care to take it to the next level."

Omid Kordestani

"It's a great thing to know you can control forces, you can be in the front, you can think out of the box to win, and you can do things that really matter."

Guy Gecht

"The other thing that I remember from my early experience was the concept that everything was doable; that it was just a question of hard work, of merit, and that any door would open."

Marc Onetto

Key Skills

- Earn unique qualifications: Success comes to people with superior intelligence and a well-rounded education. Many immigrants speak multiple languages fluently and use this to their advantage.

- Work hard: Be willing to apply yourself to the task at hand and go the extra mile. Very few people succeed in Silicon Valley working a standard 40-hour week. An understanding family helps.

- Have a relentless focus: Success in Silicon Valley is achieved by doing something different. Before Google, no one thought there was a profitable business model for search engines. Become passionate about a great idea and carry it through to completion.

Second Recipe: Strive for Excellence

"Nevertheless, it is useful to have at least one profession or skill set that you are really, really good at, because you learn perseverance, you learn to understand the depth of a field."

Aart de Geus

"I think that the company, the passion that we put behind what we do, is not superfluous, and that's what I teach to my team. Go for it. Spend the five or ten minutes: go the extra mile. That is what makes a difference."

Alex Vieux

"The balance was a challenge; I always felt I needed to work very hard. I was working harder not because I was a woman or because I was discriminated against. It was because I have this very demanding work ethic."

Aliza Peleg

Key Skills

- Inventory your skills: Have a clear understanding of what you are good at. Know your strengths. Focus on and leverage them.
- Minimize your liabilities: Hire people whose proficiencies complement yours. If you are good at engineering, team up with finance and marketing people.
- Stay on top of your game: Read the journals, research your field, network, and connect with world-class experts. Invest in your skills. Keep the blade sharp.

Third Recipe: Take a Chance—Carpe Diem!

"America gave me the chance. Of that I am convinced. You will never uproot that from my head. That's the American dream for someone who is coming from nowhere, whether it's a Jewish kid, or Black, or White, Chinese, Israeli, Ukrainian, German, whoever it is, they all have a chance. There is a day when someone says, 'Okay, show me what you can do.' In Europe, nobody says, 'Show me'."

Alex Vieux

"Because people here [U.S.] are taught to think big, they are taught to think out of the box, they are taught to take risks and they are taught to tolerate failure."

Steve Westly

"I saw very quickly that the American system was more about what you are capable of achieving, instead of where you were coming from."

Philippe Courtot

"...[There is] a skill set that's absolutely crucial, and that is to be able to make decisions on less than perfect information, and it happens all the time."

John Hennessy

"The willingness to let people fail is very important because it gives flexibility to the economy. There are something like 600,000 new enterprises started each year in the United States and most of them fail, but some don't and hope springs eternal."

George Shultz

Key Skills

- Learn to tolerate risks: Your decision to leave your country of your birth shows you are willing to embrace risk. Don't lose that edge.
- Believe in your vision: See what is possible, not what already exists.
- Be passionate: None of the people I talked with did things in half measures. All the chances they took, they were fully committed to.

Fourth Recipe: Be Daring—Just go for it!

"I would say, don't worry about your title, about the corner office, about your status. Do a great job when you get here, work with people you like to work with, surround yourself with people who inspire you, make a contribution, and then great things are going to follow."

Charly Kleissner

"Now that I am on the *dark side*, the other side [as a VC], whatever they say...you have to bet on an entrepreneur who has the enthusiasm and the guts and the get-go who wants to do it."

Henry Wong

"The biggest thing you have to have is the passion to follow your dream and you have to have the determination to convert that into something tangible."

Raj Singh

"...We just came here with six suitcases and a two year old kid and checked into a motel."

Aliza Peleg

"My father certainly instilled in me the spirit: 'Don't be afraid of anybody, and don't take crap from anybody.' My father was a real maverick."

Guy Kawasaki

Key Skills

- Believe in yourself. Take the steps to make your wildest dreams come true.

- Ignore status symbols: Many of the most successful people in the Valley dress in jeans, take their families to a Mom and Pop restaurant, and drive a hybrid car. A concern with status symbols is more typical of traditional European and Asian societies.

- Cultivate your unique brand: Dare to be different. Stick to your roots. People will remember you for who you are—not the pale imitation of a native son you might be tempted to become. In Silicon Valley, it's okay for Indians to be Indian, Chinese to be Chinese, and even people from New York can keep their New York accents.

- Cultivate your uniqueness: If reading the stories in this book teaches one thing, it should be that there is no one path to success in Silicon Valley. Dare to be different, find your own way.

Fifth Recipe: Keep at it—Push Yourself

"You can have a plan, but it's your ability, as they say, to tackle and block and to maneuver. I like to use the sailing analogy: you have to go with the wind direction, you keep making progress and you have to tack. And you have to be persistent; persistence alone wins."

Samba Murthy

"That's when I decided I wanted to go do a start-up. I knew I didn't have the experience then, nor did I have the money to start my own company back then, so I decided I first had to build up my experience. I decided to invest ten years of my time to get ready for a start-up."

Wu Fu Chen

"One main thing I learned is that success is really simply a matter of always doing better tomorrow what you do today."

Khaled Olayan

"I think it is the absolute complete, unfettered social mobility that is possible, so with certain very limited constraints, you are what you can achieve. Period!"

Nat Goldhaber

Key Skills

- Recover from failure: This is often seen as a "badge of honor" in the Valley.
- Collaborate: The many associations for foreign-born professionals are a great resource.
- Reinvent yourself: Never stop learning. Technology changes rapidly. Whatever you learned in college is now obsolete.
- Be persistent: Stay the course. Even with the fast pace at which the Valley moves, it can take time to realize your dreams.

Sixth Recipe: Be Aware

"You have to become really aware of the cultural differences and if you're not aware of them, you're not going to be able to work well in this society. You have to look at yourself and understand your own culture to be able to understand others'. Mix up the pictures, don't stay with what you're most comfortable with."

Arno Penzias

"In a multicultural environment, 'careful observation' is a challenge that may sometimes be required to understand cultural metaphors beyond what we are traditionally used to."

Rajesh Gupta

Key Skills

- Be culturally aware: Not only of American customs and manners, but also of the many different cultures that you will meet working in Silicon Valley.
- Be aware of the needs of your family: High-tech "work/life balance" does not match what other cultures, or even other parts of America, accept as normal. However, you need to make time for your family and keep it in your plans.
- Be aware of others: Including the value that your staff, colleagues and mentors can offer. No one succeeds alone. Be willing to ask questions to make sure you understand what others can offer to help in the success of your project.

Seventh Recipe: Be a Leader

"An effective leader in a multi-national cultural setting probably says something like: 'Hey, I will do my best to bring people that I believe can be the future leaders of this company. I will do my very best to train them with whatever the company has accumulated anywhere, and give them the base level of knowledge, I'll give them the best connections possible and then I'll unleash them to the market.' I think that lacking that realization is often what prevents people from being an okay manager or an okay leader to becoming a great leader. It is about total empowerment, it is cultural appreciation at such a thorough level, that you are willing to give it up."

Allen Wang

"One of the biggest challenges to leadership is that it is so easy to believe that everybody has the same DNA and to treat them all the same, as opposed to really understanding what motivates people and how they would like to be treated."

Shantanu Narayen

"When you become a CEO, the key to being successful is actually to pick up what the right decision is, not to be right."

Guy Gecht

"For me, the first most important characteristic of a leader is to be able to listen, and define an action plan that empowers the maximum of employees."

Marylene Delbourg Delphis

Key Skills

- Develop self-understanding: Leaders know their own strengths and weaknesses, when they can accomplish something alone and when they need to ask for help.

- Embody the vision of the company or the project: Whether you lead a team or a whole company, the people you work with need to be inspired by your example. An authoritarian style of leadership is uncommon in Silicon Valley. Collaborative, inspiring leaders have been the norm since Hewlett and Packard established the "HP Way" in the 1950s.

- Set the direction: As well as embodying an inspiring vision, leaders excel at execution. In the fast paced, high-tech world, decisions need to be made often and fast. Most of our interviewees live at a fast pace and don't shy away from making quick calls.

Eighth Recipe: Be Innovative

"The biggest challenge, to be quite honest with you, was getting the Internet into operation."

Vinton Cerf

"I was proposing to the company to do something audacious which had not been done before."

Suhas Patil

"If you can present an idea, a concept, a technical piece that excels—you win. I don't care who you are, you're Martian, I don't care."

Henry Wong

"Because life is not just spice and curry, you know. There are other things, so keep an open mind."

Samba Murthy

Key Skills

- Develop your creativity: Have fun at work. Look for the playful aspects of your projects. Look for new ways to do things.
- Think differently: Use your experience as an immigrant "outsider" to your advantage and look at issues from a different angle. Don't be afraid to challenge the assumptions in your industry.
- Broaden your horizons: Many foreign-born professionals stick with social groups from their native countries. Step outside the box and take every opportunity to meet people from other cultures and backgrounds.
- Cultivate your curiosity: Be relentlessly curious about your own industry, other industries and other cultures. Network and attend trade shows. You never know where the next innovative idea will come from.

Ninth Recipe: Be Passionate

"I always had a very intense desire to do exactly what I wanted to do, both in coming to this country and starting the companies that I did. This is still true for me today. My passion in life, if you will, is to build better products."

Andy Bechtolsheim

"I think if you pursue things that you are interested in and you work very hard at them and you're passionate about them, you'll probably be successful IF you have selected a good environment."

Miriam Rivera

"I love what I do and if you get a lot of satisfaction and reward from what you do, time goes by quickly."

Qi Lu

"I love what I do, I do what I love **and** I get paid for it."

Jean-Louis Gassée

Key Skills

- Put passion into every aspect of your work: The trick is not just to feel passionately about your job, but to act passionately too.
- Renew your passion: Think back to what your original goal was. Peel off the layers. Get back to your first instincts, recall what you wanted to accomplish.
- Look for new solutions—passionately: Keep the dynamics alive. The people around you will catch the same bug you have.
- Be inspired by others: Seek out people who are passionate about their work and spend time with them.

Tenth Recipe: Build a Network

"Networking is a very important success factor."

Dina Bitton

"It's a small place. A lot of us know each other. We worked for one another at one time or the other, we have competed, we have cooperated."

Vinton Cerf

"It's [success] a self-fulfilling prophecy when you surround yourself with successful people."

Chi Foon Chan

"To be a successful leader, your people have to be successful with you. This is the only way to lead to success—and you cannot do it alone."

Khaled Olayan

Key Skills

- Never stop networking: Just as this book was written as a result of networking, so should you cultivate your network from the day you arrive here. Make it a continuous process.
- Pay it forward: Don't just join a network looking for what you can get out of it. Make real contributions and rewards will come.
- Network online: There are a growing number of online networks such as LinkedIn, Facebook and others. Be selective with whom you link, but grow your network.
- Develop superior networking skills: Don't keep information close to the vest, work with others, include them; together you will guarantee each other's successes and growth.
- Invest in collaborative decision-making and project development. Don't be a lone wolf. Teamwork is key to success.

Eleventh Recipe: Give Back

"At a young age, success is if you meet your goals. You set goals for yourself and, if you meet them, or go beyond them, you are successful. At a later age, that is not sufficient; you want to leave your mark on society by giving back and improving life around you."

Dan Maydan

"If you combine the skills, the mindset, the culture with the financial contribution, you can accomplish great things with relatively few resources [talking about his philanthropic work, IVN, in Israel]. It was very satisfying to see that we could do this—a bunch of high-tech CEOs. We did not claim any expertise in education, we were able to put our minds together and solve this problem."

Eric Benhamou

"Money is a part of life and it is necessary to make money, but when you have made that money, what can you do with it? The only thing you can do is to give it away. And give it away, because that is the way you can influence and guide things that happen in society. So if you make money beyond your own needs, then you are in a position to contribute in a philanthropic way."

Suhas Patil

"I had this sense from early childhood that to be successful in life, one must do something that will outlast one's lifetime and leave an impact for the future."

Rajesh Gupta

"This can be done [creating a global foundation] through education, providing rights for women—especially providing empowerment for women—using microcredit cooperatives and computers to educate women and their children. Then the whole world becomes a lot better."

Kamran Elahian

Key Skills

- Give early and give often: In 1940, when HP had been in business less than a year, Bill Hewlett and Dave Packard gave their first check to charity. Don't wait until you are a millionaire to give back.

- Give your time as well as money: There's no better way to serve the community than by volunteering through a local service club or community organization.

- Make a difference: You have a unique opportunity to balance your work-life with meaningful personal rewards when you make a difference in someone's life.

- Use your best skills: Non-profits often need the managerial, technical and leadership skills you hone at work.

Twelfth Recipe: Have Fun, Enjoy the Ride

"For me, I'm a little bit happy-go-lucky. I enjoy the journey."

Chi Foon Chan

[To the question: Are you having fun?] "Oh, yes, I am! Talk about really connecting the whole world together! All of my companies give people the technology to enable mobility—to connect and exchange ideas."

Kamran Elahian

"We then spent most of our energies protecting what we have, instead of thinking of how we could better enjoy and grow to better enjoy what we have and grow a better future for us all."

Philippe Courtot

Key Skills

- Enjoy the ride: Don't focus only on the end result, enjoy where you are today. Take the time to stop and smell the roses.

- Don't lose sight of the little things: Take pleasure in the details that make your life enjoyable. Take breaks. Enjoy your surroundings. If you are new to Silicon Valley, take a day trip to the Santa Cruz Mountains and Half Moon Bay.

- Work hard and play hard: Have fun with your family and friends around you. It is important to include them in your journey.

Policy Implications

Many immigrants arrive in the U.S. on either foreign student or H-1B visas. H-1B visas are temporary visas used to hire skilled foreign nationals for up to six years. While both have historically allowed significant numbers of immigrants to enter the U.S., these circumstances are changing.

Security issues since 9/11 have slowed down the rate at which foreign students are choosing to enter the U.S. It is claimed that, "Visa requirements imposed on foreign students since the Sept. 11 terrorist attacks are confusing, redundant and causing more problems than they solve." [17]

Congress has not allocated a sufficient number of H-1B visas. In 9 of the past 11 years, employers have used up the entire quota of H-1B visas prior to the end of the fiscal year. This year, 2007, the H-1B visas were gone the same day they were made available, such was the rush.

The danger, as identified by the NVCA report, is that, "The brightest minds worldwide are willing to neither wait nor put up with the uncertainty. They are going to other places, including Australia, Canada and Europe." [18]

It is obvious that if Silicon Valley (and the greater U.S.) is to maintain its competitive edge, immigration restrictions currently in place must be lifted. The current policy is "indiscriminate and affects our ability to attract the talent that the valley needs." [19]

---

17. Boulard, G., "Black Issues in Higher Education," 'Foreign student visa process clumsy and cumbersome, educators say,' 2004. Ref: http://findarticles.com/p/articles/mi_m0DXK/is_19_21/ai_n8964634

18. Anderson, S. and M. Platzer, American Made: The Impact of Immigrant Entrepreneurs and Professionals on U.S. Competitiveness, National Venture Capital Association (NVCA), 2006, 11.

19. Koo, G., "On Immigration: Silicon Valley needs immigrant minds," New America Media, February 16, 2006. Ref: http://sfgate.com/cgi-bin/article.cgi?file=/chronicle/archive/2006/02/16/EDGU9GJE5F1.DTL

Hopefully, anyone reading this book outside the U.S., who wishes to immigrate, or come to work here, will be able to find a solution and secure a visa. This is the first hurdle to overcome.

Closing Thoughts

"...nobody is great without work...There's no evidence of high level performance without experience or practice. Reinforcing that no-free-lunch finding is vast evidence that even the most accomplished people need around ten years of hard work before becoming world-class, a pattern so well established researchers call it the ten-year rule."

"What it takes to be great," Geoffrey Colvin,
***Fortune Magazine*, October 30, 2006** [20]

"If I could say just one thing about Silicon Valley, this is it: every generation that came before us had to make a choice in life between pursuing a steady career and pursuing wild adventures. In Silicon Valley, that trade-off has been recircuited. By injecting mind-boggling amounts of risk into the once stodgy domain of gray-suited business, young people no longer have to choose. It's a two-for-one deal: the career path has become an adventure into the unknown. More happens here and so quickly, satisfying anybody's craving for newness. In six months you might get a job, be laid off, start a company, sell it, become a consultant, who knows?"

***The Nudist on The Late Shift*, Po Bronson**[21]

Silicon Valley is a place to realize your dreams. It's a place where the journey is as rewarding as the destination. The people I interviewed all mirrored this attitude. They were interested in the way they do things, in the innovation they were part of, and not necessarily in the outcome. This is easy for them, you might say, since they have truly "Made It!"

---

20. Colvin, G., "What it takes to be great," Fortune Magazine, October 30, 2006. Ref: http://money.cnn.com/magazines/fortune/fortune_archive/2006/10/30/8391794/index.htm

21. Bronson, P., The Nudist on the Late Shift: And Other True Tales of Silicon Valley, Random House, New York, NY, 1999, xxvii.

But it's precisely this approach that helped them "make it." If you can't cultivate this mindset, you might be better staying in Bordeaux, Bangalore or Beijing.

Silicon Valley is a small place where people know each other, and depend on each other to get things done. This is also a place where friendship and helping people is important. It's important to safeguard your reputation. The people in your network will quickly hear if you weren't up front.

The Valley relies on networks—business, friendship, collaboration, the old guys helping out the new, younger ones. Don't abuse the trust of the people you meet socially or at work.

But above all, Silicon Valley is a unique place where the opportunity to be great and do great things is alive and well. Now that you've read this book, won't you join in?

Appendix

A List of Possible Questions to Ask

How would you describe what you are doing professionally today?

How did your childhood experiences and/or your family influence your choice of career?

What role did your education play in what you are currently doing?

What were some of the biggest obstacles/challenges you had to overcome to be successful?

What does it mean to you to be successful?

What factors contributed to your success?

Could you have become as successful outside of the Silicon Valley (or did this environment give you something you can't find elsewhere)?

Does your background as a Frenchman/Chinese/Indian etc. give you unique advantages as a leader in your company?

Or, how does your foreign background affect where you are today?

Has the window of opportunity closed in the Silicon Valley and opened elsewhere?

What are the greatest challenges for multicultural leadership today?

What three things are most important to keep in mind to be a great leader?

What are the three things to never do as a leader?

What advice would you give (Indians, Chinese, French, etc.) who are either living here or coming here to work?

Do you have anyone else you can suggest I talk to?

Appendix

B Universities Interviewees Attended

- Ben Gurion University, Israel
- Bowling Green State University, U.S.
- Carnegie Mellon, U.S
- Case Western, U.S.
- Columbia University, U.S.
- Cornell University, U.S.
- École Central, France
- École Nationale Supérieure des Télécommunications, France
- Fudan University, China
- Georgetown, U.S.
- Golden Gate University, U.S.
- IIT, Delhi, India
- IIT, Kanpur, India
- McMaster University, Canada
- MIT, U.S.

- Osmania University, India
- Paris (Orsay) University, France
- Polytechnical Institute, Singapore
- Princeton University, U.S.
- Rutgers University, U.S.
- SMU, U.S.
- Stanford University, U.S.
- State University of New York at Buffalo, U.S.
- State University of New York at Stony Brook, U.S.
- Technion Institute, Israel
- Technische Universitaet, Germany
- Tel Aviv University, Israel
- Tsinghua University, China
- UC Berkeley, U.S.
- UC Davis, U.S.
- UCLA, U.S.
- University of Edinburgh, United Kingdom
- Vienna University of Technology, Austria
- Weizmann Institute, Israel

About the Author

Angelika Blendstrup, Ph.D., is the founder and principal of Blendstrup & Associates.[22] She specializes in individualized, intercultural business communications training, accent reduction, and presentation skill coaching. She works with international as well as U.S. executives to assist them in improving their written and oral communications skills, and prepares them how to write and give effective presentations.

22. http://www.professional-business-communications.com

Angelika holds a Ph.D. in Bilingual, Bicultural Education from Stanford University. She speaks five languages and has taught U.S. business communications skills to international executives both privately as well as in companies in the Silicon Valley such as DreamWorks, Sun Microsystems, Microsoft, Oracle and Cisco.

Angelika teaches classes at Stanford University on topics such as cross cultural communication, managing virtual teams and the art of interviewing successfully.

Angelika is the Co-President of *InterFrench Silicon Valley (SiliconFrench)* whose goal is to merge the best features of the French and American cultures.

She is also a Co-Executive Editor of the *Happy About International Business Communications* series. Angelika can be reached at angelika.blendstrup@gmail.com.

Books

Other Happy About® Books

Purchase these books at Happy About
http://happyabout.info
or at other online and physical bookstores.

Increase your Effectiveness in the American Business Environment

Presentations, meetings, phone calls, and more—this book covers all you need to know to effectively communicate in the American workplace.

Paperback $19.95
eBook $11.95

Learn the rules of successful online networking!

Whether you are a novice or expert online networker, there are tips and techniques in this book you can immediately put to use.

Paperback $19.95
eBook $11.95

Projects are MESSY!

From the minute the project begins, all manner of changes, surprises and disasters befall them. Unfortunately most of these are PREDICTABLE and AVOIDABLE.

Paperback $19.95
eBook $11.95

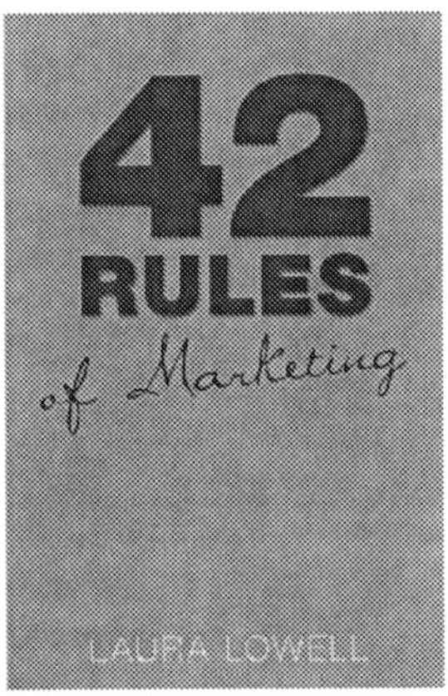

Learn the 42 Rules of Marketing!

Compilation of ideas, theories and practical approaches to marketing challenges that marketers know they should do, but don't always have the time or patience for.

Paperback $19.95
eBook $11.95

A message from the author

From my blog at http://businessspeak.wordpress.com:

Over the past year and a half, I have come to know many successful foreign-born as well as American entrepreneurs and have learned a great deal from them. Many other foreign-born professionals are pursuing success in Silicon Valley in the field of information technology (IT), and even more hope to come to the United States to study and to learn the American way of doing business.

Do you have any advice for these foreign-born IT professionals hoping to "make it" in America? Are you willing to share your own success story? Being able to learn from your experience can be of great value to others.

Of course, each of us measures success in our own way. What does success mean to you? Professionally? Personally? Do you believe you have achieved success? What was your path? What was difficult? Easy? Even surprising?

If you have a story to tell, or if you know someone whose story would be of value and interest to others, please feel free to:

- Contribute your comments to my blog: http://businessspeak.wordpress.com
- Send me an email so I can contact you directly to hear more: angelika.blendstrup@gmail.com

I am interested in writing another book that will present stories from the next generation of entrepreneurs. Also in the coming months, I will begin podcasting interviews on my blog with such professionals.

Printed in the United States
202446BV00003B/132/A

9 781600 050756